FAITH CLINIC

VOLUME XXIX

-PANIC ATTACKS EDITION –

When Your Spirit Says "Trust God," But Your Body Hits The Emergency Button.

DR. PATRICIA S. TANNER

IBG Publications, Inc.

DR. PATRICIA S. TANNER

Published by I.B.G. Publications, Inc., a Power to Wealth Company

Web address: www.ibgpublications.com

admin@ibgpublications.com / 904-419-9810

Copyright, 2026 by Patricia S. Tanner

IBG Publications, Inc., Jacksonville, FL

ISBN: 978-1-971850-17-7

Tanner, Patricia S.

Faith Clinic, Volume XXIX-Panic Attack Edition- *When Your Spirit Says "Trust God," But Your Body Hits The Emergency Button*

Printed in the United States of America.

DEDICATION

This book is dedicated to the strong ones who get tired of being strong. To the ones who learned how to survive every storm but forgot how to rest afterward. To every overachiever, fixer, planner, rescuer, and "I'm fine" specialist who secretly prayed *"God, I just want to be free."*

You are the reason this Clinic exists. You're the patients who walk, in confident and walk out changed. May these pages remind you that surrender is not weakness, it's wisdom. And that dependence on God isn't a downgrade, it's deliverance.

This is for you, the independent hearts learning how to heal under new management.

Your Faith Practitioner and friend,

DR. PATRICIA S. TANNER
The Faith Doctor

ACKNOWLEDGMENTS

To my Great Physician, Dr. Jesus, thank You for writing every chapter before I lived it. For refusing to let me self-diagnose my pain or medicate my pride. For calling me back when I mistook control for courage, and independence for identity.

To the Holy Spirit, my Counselor and Care Partner, thank You for every whisper, every nudge, every quiet correction that shaped these pages into healing. You are the steady voice in my chaos.

To my family, thank you for loving me through every rewrite, every late night, and every emotional ICU moment of this book's creation. You are my first ministry and my forever reminder that healing is a group project.

To every reader who's ever walked through their own faith rehab, thank you for showing up to your own recovery. You are proof that God still specializes in stubborn patients.

And finally, to every woman and man who's ever looked in the mirror and said, "I shouldn't still be here"… You're right, but grace decided otherwise.

TABLE OF CONTENTS

Why Your Spirit Trusts God but Your Body Never Got the Memo

PART III: TREATMENT: PRACTICAL + SPIRITUAL PEACE REBUILDERS

EPILOGUE: You're Not Broken, You're Being Rebuilt

✓ FAITH CLINIC INTAKE FORM

(Patient Name: Believer Who Panics but Still Trusts God)
Chief Complaint:
☐ "My chest is tight."
☐ "My thoughts won't stop yelling."
☐ "My heart is playing the drums again."
☐ "I'm afraid of things that don't exist."
☐ "Everything is fine but my body disagrees."
☐ "All of the above, send help.

When did symptoms start?
☐ Childhood
☐ Adolescence
☐ After that one traumatic event
☐ Randomly out of nowhere like a jump-scare
☐ Yesterday
☐ During worship (of course)

What makes the symptoms worse?
☐ Overthinking
☐ Being alone
☐ Being around people
☐ Deep teachings
☐ Unexpected bills
☐ The group chat going silent unexpectedly
☐ The enemy
☐ Coffee (let's be honest)

What helps, even if just a little?
☐ Prayer
☐ Slow breathing
☐ Worship music
☐ Laying on the floor like a Christian burrito
☐ Reminding myself I'm not dying

□ Talking to God mid-panic
□ Not Googling symptoms

Describe your faith level:
□ Mustard seed
□ Mustard seed with water
□ Depends on the day
□ I love Jesus but my nervous system is a hater

Spiritual Vitals:
Heart: □ racing □ trembling □ confused but trying
Mind: □ spiraling □ tired □ begging for peace
Spirit: □ still standing □ whispering "trust God" □ exhausted but faithful

Treatment Goals:
□ To not feel like I'm dying every Tuesday
□ Return to normal breathing
□ Learn how to trust God *and* calm my body
□ Stop rehearsing worst-case scenarios
□ Heal what triggered this in the first place
□ Live free, fully, peacefully, spiritually grounded

Physician's Note:
You're not crazy.
You're not faithless.
You're not alone.
Your nervous system is loud, but God is louder.
Proceed to the Waiting Room.

✓ WAITING ROOM PAGE

"Please Remain Calm… Or Try To."
Welcome to the Faith Clinic Waiting Room, where anxious believers gather, clutching their chests, pretending they're fine, and scrolling on social media until their name is called. You're safe here. No judgment. No weird looks. Just a room full of people whose bodies overreact to life like it's an Olympic sport.
While you wait:

☑ Breathe (slowly).
In through your nose like you're smelling something expensive. Out through your mouth like you're blowing out birthday candles you don't want to admit you're too old for.

☑ Remind yourself:
- You are not alone in your panic.
- God isn't annoyed with your nervous system.
- Nothing is wrong with you; something happened *to* you.
- Peace is still possible, even mid-shake.

☑ Read the posters on the wall:
- "Your Anxiety Is Loud. God Is Louder."
- "You're Not Dying, You're Just Dramatic (It's Okay)."
- "Jesus Calms Storms… Even the Ones Inside Your Ribcage."
- "Breathe. Your Spirit Knows the Way Home."

☑ What to do while you wait:
- Wiggle your toes, it interrupts panic loops.
- Put your hand on your chest and say, "We are safe."
- Don't rehearse your funeral. It's not your time.
- Whisper a scripture even if your voice shakes.

Soon, you'll be called into the exam room, not for judgment, but for healing.

Reflections

✚ FAITH CLINIC WRISTBAND PAGE

(Print, cut, or save to remind yourself of your identity during storms.)

FAITH CLINIC: PATIENT ID WRISTBAND

NAME: ____

CONDITION: Anxiety, Panic Episodes, Nervous System Recalibration

TREATMENT: Worship, Naming, Community, Breath Regulation, Holy Spirit

STATUS: Healing in Progress: Do Not Disturb the Miracle

NOTES:

• Patient is not weak.

• Symptoms do not equal failure.

• Storms do not own this patient.

• God remains present at all times.

ATTENDING PHYSICIAN: JESUS, PRINCE OF PEACE

HOSPITAL: THE KINGDOM OF GOD

ROOM: "Under the Shadow of the Almighty" (Psalm 91)

PERSONAL NOTES

12

INTRODUCTION

There are moments in life when you don't need a medical degree to know something is wrong. Your body will tell you. Loudly. Dramatically. Without warning. In the most inconvenient places, the grocery store, the church lobby, or the moment the pastor says, "Turn to your neighbor."

Suddenly your chest forgets it's Christian. Your thoughts start preaching a sermon no one asked for. Your hands get sweaty enough to baptize someone. And your heart is doing the absolute most, pounding, racing, doing backflips like it's auditioning for a gymnastics team you never signed up for. Meanwhile, your spirit, the part of you that loves Jesus, sings worship songs, knows scripture, and has seen God come through, is calmly repeating: ***"Trust God. You're okay."***

But your body is like: ***"Girl, call 911. This is the end."*** And that is where this book begins. Not in calm places. Not in confident moments. Not in the fully healed, emotionally stable, social-media-polished parts of your story. This book begins in chaos. It begins with shaking. It begins in the bathroom stall at church where you're whispering, *"God, what is happening to me?"* It begins on the kitchen floor when your chest tightens and your legs feel numb and you're convinced this is the end, again, but something deeper in you still whispers, "Trust Me." This book begins where your faith and your biology collide.

THE MOMENT YOU REALIZED YOUR BODY DIDN'T GET THE MEMO

There is something humbling, almost embarrassing, about feeling your body panic while your spirit is trying to stay saved. You can quote every scripture you've ever learned. You can speak in tongues until your jaw gets tired. But your body? Your body will interrupt you in the middle of a sermon with, "Hey, I don't feel safe. Let's freak out." No warning. No reason. No context. Just a full-blown emergency siren inside your chest like you've been drafted into a war you did not enlist in. And here's what nobody tells you: You can love God and still have panic attacks. You can trust God and still have a nervous system that overreacts like a toddler who missed naptime. You can have strong faith and a shaky body at the same time. You can be anointed and anxious. Saved and spiraling. Spiritual and sweating. You are not broken. You are not faithless. You are not weak. You are human. Your nervous system is doing its job, even when it's using the wrong data.

THE LIES YOU'VE BEEN TOLD OF ABOUT PANIC

Let's go ahead and expose them:

Lie #1: "If you trusted God more, you wouldn't panic."
Incorrect. Moses panicked. Elijah panicked. David panicked so hard he wrote a whole book about it.

Lie #2: "Just pray about it."
Yes, prayer works. But your nervous system also has a voice, a memory, a trauma library, and a biological reaction time faster than your favorite worship song.

<u>Lie #3</u>: "Christians shouldn't struggle with anxiety."
Christians shouldn't sin either but look how that's going.

<u>Lie #4</u>: "This is a demon."
Some things are spiritual. Some things are chemical. Some things are both. But either way, God is Lord over all of it.

<u>Lie #5</u>: "You should be stronger by now."
Healing isn't linear. Growth isn't instant. And God never asked you to pretend you're invincible.

THE TRUTH YOU'VE NEVER BEEN TOLD ENOUGH

You can panic and still walk in purpose. You can tremble and still trust God. You can feel fear and not be ruled by it. You can struggle with your biology and still live a supernatural life.

The presence of panic does not prove the absence of faith. If anything, it shows your faith even more, because it takes courage to keep trusting God when your body is screaming the opposite. You are not disqualified. You are not disowned. You are not disfavored. You are simply in the part of the story where God stabilizes what life destabilized. And He's not intimidated by your symptoms.

THE GOSPEL ACCORDING TO SWEATY PALMS AND RACING HEARTS

Let's rewrite the narrative. Your panic is not the villain. Your panic is the alarm system telling you something in your story needs tending. Not condemning. Not ignoring. Not shaming.

Tending.

Your panic is the invitation to slow down, breathe, listen, and let God walk into the parts of you that you've tried to out-pray, out-shout, or out-perform. Your panic is where your humanity meets His compassion. Where your trauma meets His truth. Where your shaking meets His steadiness. Where your breathlessness meets His breath. Your symptoms are not signs of God's absence; they are invitations into His closeness.

WHY THIS BOOK EXISTS

This book is not a guilt trip. This is not the "stop being dramatic" manual. This is not the "pray it away in 30 seconds" fantasy Christianity that leaves people feeling spiritually defective.

This book is about a clinic. A holy hospital. Where faith and psychology sit side-by-side. Where prayer meets the parasympathetic nervous system. Where scripture meets the science of trauma. Where the Holy Spirit meets the hyperventilating believer and says, **"I am here. Breathe."**

This is the book for:
- Believers whose bodies lie to them
- Christians who panic in private but look brave in public
- Worship leaders who hold microphones with trembling hands
- Pastors who preach peace while fighting anxiety
- Teens who think panic means they're broken
- Adults who pretend they're strong because they don't want to look weak
- Everyone who has ever said, "I trust God… so why does my body feel like this?"

You are not reading this because you failed. You are reading this because you're healing.

WHAT THIS BOOK WILL DO FOR YOU

It will help you:
- Understand panic without shame
- Rebuild peace in your nervous system
- Connect body + spirit instead of letting them fight

- Use scripture as strategy, not band-aids
- Heal triggers you stopped recognizing
- Develop practices that calm your body and strengthen your faith
- Learn how to trust God with your biology, not just your beliefs
- Stop fearing your symptoms
- Prepare for moments when panic tries to return
- Live freely, fully, bravely, peacefully

This book will give you tools, spiritual, emotional, neurological, and practical, to face panic without losing yourself. This book will teach you the language your body speaks and the language your spirit responds to.

This book will walk you through the messy, real, unpolished parts of healing, with humor, honesty, and holy wisdom. This book will not shame you. This book will not rush you. This book will not demand you be "stronger." This book will hold your hand and say: **"Breathe. God is here. You're safe. Let's walk through this together."**

THE PROMISE YOU CAN HOLD

Healing is possible. Peace is possible. Rest is possible. Breathing again is possible. Stability is possible. Life without constant alarms is possible. You will not panic forever. Your body will not overpower your spirit. Your symptoms will not win the war God already declared victory over.

This book is your training ground. Your reset. Your restoration. Your rehabilitation clinic for the anxious parts of your soul. And on the last page, you will say with confidence:

"My body tried to scare me, but God stayed with me. I didn't die. I didn't drown. I didn't break beyond repair. I learned to breathe

again." This is your turning point. This is your clinic. This is your healing. Let's begin.

Reflections

Chapter 1:

WHEN YOUR BODY FILES AN EMERGENCY ALERT FOR NO REASON

SYMPTOM: "My body is screaming danger, but nothing is actually wrong."

There is a specific kind of panic that feels like betrayal, not the betrayal of another person, but the betrayal of your own body. It starts subtly, with a flutter in the chest or a tightness under your ribs, barely noticeable enough to name but familiar enough to fear. Then, without invitation or explanation, that flutter becomes a warning siren. Your heart begins racing like it's being chased through your ribcage, your breathing decides to file for early retirement, and your nervous system starts sending out evacuation notices as if a hurricane just touched down in your bloodstream. Meanwhile, you are standing in the produce aisle at the grocery store or sitting in church minding your sanctified business wondering, *"What in the holy world is happening to me right now?"* 

The worst part is that nothing around you explains it. No threat. No danger. No crisis. Just normal life being lived, while your body acts like it's starring in a dramatic survival movie where it plays both the villain and the victim. Your hands tremble with a fear that has no source. Your legs feel unstable even though nothing is physically wrong. Your mind begins whispering catastrophic lies like, "You're dying," or "You're losing control," or "This is the big one." All while your logical side tries its best to reason with chaos but quickly gets drowned out by adrenaline screaming for attention. It feels humiliating, terrifying, confusing, and exhausting, all at the same time.

This is the symptom: **your body initiating a full-scale emergency even when your life is perfectly safe.** It is the experience of having your biology behave as if danger is near when danger is nowhere to be found. It is the heartbreak of watching your own physical responses contradict everything your spirit knows, believes, and trusts about God. And no matter how much you tell yourself, "Calm down, nothing is wrong," your body keeps reacting like everything is wrong. It's not rebellion. It's not a lack of faith. It's a system out of alignment reacting to old wounds with new alarms.

TEACHING: Your Body Remembers What Your Spirit Has Forgotten, But God Can Heal Both

Before you judge yourself, before you label yourself weak, before you let shame convince you that you're spiritually failing, you need to hear this truth: *your body is not your enemy, it's your messenger.* Panic is not always logical, but it is always communicating something. Your body has its own memory bank, its own trauma archive, its own alarm system built from every injury, disappointment, harm, and fear you've survived. While your spirit has been transformed and renewed by God, your body may still be operating off the survival codes it created long before you knew peace was even possible.

Your panic is not random. It is not stupid. It is not weakness. It is a protective system that teaches to anticipate danger long before you could articulate what danger even meant. Sometimes your nervous system responds to a smell, a tone of voice, a memory, a posture, or even a shift in the environment that reminds it of a past wound. And because your nervous system does not have the gift of discernment, it reacts with the intensity of the original trauma even when the present moment is completely safe.

Spiritually, this feels like betrayal, because you know God is with you, yet your body is reacting like you are alone. You know you're safe, yet your heart races like you're trapped. You know the truth, yet your breath refuses to cooperate. But here is the gospel  truth buried beneath the layers of trembling muscles and shortness of breath: *you can trust God while your body is having a biological*

meltdown. The panic in your body does not cancel the faith in your spirit. Both can exist at the same time, and God does not condemn you for the distance between them.

Jesus Himself showed us that the body and spirit do not always align instantly. In Gethsemane, His spirit was surrendered, but His body sweated drops of blood under the pressure of what was coming. This is not a sign of faithlessness; it is the reality of carrying human biology inside spiritual identity. God never asked you to pretend your body is already perfected. He asks you to invite Him into the moments when your body is overwhelmed, because He is master over every heartbeat, every muscle, every breath, and every nervous system response.

 Healing begins not when panic stops, but when you stop shaming yourself for having a human body. Healing begins when you offer God, you're trembling instead of hiding it. Healing begins when you allow your symptoms to become signals, not of doom, but of areas where God is ready to breathe peace, truth, and restoration into the parts of you that have been living on high alert for far too long.

Your panic is not a sign that God abandoned you. It is the place where God plans to meet you next.

FAITH PRESCRIPTION

1. Take this truth daily: "I am not in danger. My body is reacting to a memory, not a moment. God is here, and I am safe."

2. When panic rises, whisper scripture instead of diagnosis:
- "He restores my soul." (Psalm 23:3)
- "The Lord is the strength of my life, of whom shall I be afraid?" (Psalm 27:1)
- "Peace, be still." (Mark 4:39)

These scriptures don't magically silence panic, but they anchor your spirit while your body recalibrates.

3. Engage the breath God gave you: Breathe in for 4 seconds. Hold for 4. Exhale for 6. Tell your body, "We are not under attack."
4. Place your hand on your chest: Feel your heartbeat. Say, "You are safe. God is with us. Slow down."

5. Limit Google. Increase grace. WebMD is not your spiritual gift. Let God lead before fear informs.

HOLY SPIRIT CONSULT

The Holy Spirit whispers what panic tries to drown out: **"I am with you in every breath. You are not alone in your shaking. I hold your heart steady even when you feel out of control."** He does not shout over your symptoms; He sits inside them with you. He reminds you that the God who calmed the sea still calms nervous systems. He brings back to your memory the truth you forget when panic gets loud. He speaks peace into the places where your body feels abandoned. And He guides you into the slow, steady healing you never believed was possible. Your body may sound the alarm, but the Holy Spirit is the One who turns it off.

GUIDED PRAYER

"Father, I come to You with honesty, not performance. My body is overwhelmed. My heart is racing. My breath is unsteady. But I choose You in this moment. I surrender every symptom, every fear, every false alarm. Teach my body what my spirit already knows that I am safe in You. Calm the panic that rises without cause. Quiet the storms inside of me. Let Your peace over rides every racing thought an override sling muscle. I trust You even when my body disagrees. And I thank You because You never leave me alone in the shaking. Amen."

REFLECTION PAGE

- What does my body usually feel before panic starts?

____

____

____

- What lies did my panic tell me today?

____

____

____

- What truth did God whisper in response?

____

____

____

- What places or people make my body tense even when I feel spiritually fine?

____

____

____

- What would it look like to give God access to my physical reactions, not just my spiritual desires?

DOCTOR'S ORDERS

✓ Your symptoms are real, but they are not fatal.

✓ Your panic is loud, but God is louder.

✓ You are allowed to be human and still believe God completely.

✓ Practice breathing when you're calm so your body remembers it when you're not.

✓ Stop explaining your panic to people who lack spiritual depth or emotional intelligence.

✓ Keep showing up, healing takes time.

✓ You're not dying. You're healing. Keep going.

DR. PATRICIA S. TANNER

PERSONAL NOTES

26

Chapter 2:

YOUR CHEST IS PREACHING DOOM BUT YOUR SPIRIT IS WHISPERING "PEACE"

SYMPTOM: "My chest keeps sending danger signals even though my spirit knows God is here."

It's one of the strangest contradictions you can experience as a believer: everything in your environment is calm, nothing is wrong,  nothing is threatening, nothing is spiraling, and yet your chest tightens like you just received the worst news of your life. It starts with that familiar pressure, like someone placed a weight on your sternum without your permission. Then the ache floods in not the ache of sadness, not the ache of heartbreak, but the ache of fear… a fear that has no reason, no source, and no logic behind it. You sit still, you pray, you breathe, you focus, you repeat scripture, but your chest is convinced something catastrophic is about to happen.

Your chest becomes its own prophet of doom. It preaches panic. It delivers warnings. It declares that something is wrong even when everything is right. But at the same time, often at the *exact* same moment, your spirit is whispering peace. It's quietly reminding you, *"This isn't danger. This is sensation. This is fear without fact. This is your body responding to something old, not something now."* Your chest is loud, but your spirit is steady. Your chest screams, "You're not safe." Your spirit whispers, "You are covered." Your body rings eight alarms. Your spirit lights one candle.

And this tug-of-war leaves you exhausted. You feel torn between the God you trust and the body you live in, between what you believe and what you physically feel. It is painful to watch your chest behave like tragedy is unfolding while your spirit is calmly anchored in truth. You begin to question yourself: *Am I missing something? Is this spiritual warfare? Am I under attack? Am I being warned?* But deep down, you know the truth, your body is simply overwhelmed, and overwhelmed bodies exaggerate fear.

This is the symptom: your chest becoming a false prophet of danger, while your spirit tries to anchor you in peace. The contradiction feels unbearable, but you are not broken, you are human, and you're learning how to align the voice of your body with the voice of your God.

TEACHING: Your Chest Feels What Your Past Taught It, Your Spirit Follows What God Taught It

The chest is one of the most sensitive places in the human body, physically and emotionally. It holds your heart, your lungs, your breath, your voice, your vulnerability, your capacity for connection, and your deepest memories of pain. It is no surprise, then, that the chest is the first place to respond when fear rises. It tightens when you're overwhelmed, constricts when you feel unsafe, and aches when memories are triggered that your mind no longer consciously remembers.

The chest reacts fast, faster than your thoughts, faster than your logic, faster than your scriptures. It reacts based on memory, not  theology. It reacts from history, not holiness. It reacts from every moment your heart was broken, every moment you felt unsafe, every moment fear taught you to brace yourself for the worst. Your chest does not care how many verses you know, it cares about survival. It is not trying to betray you; it is trying to prepare you.

But your spirit operates differently. Your spirit does not rely on experience; it relies on truth. It does not follow memory, it follows revelation. It does not respond to fear; it responds to God. So, while your chest is reacting to old wounds with new pressure, your spirit is steady in the truth that God is near, God is present, God is able, God is covering you, God is for you, and God is not leaving you in this moment of panic.

This contradiction is not evidence of a weak believer; it is evidence of a believer walking through the tension of being both spiritual and biological. Your spirit has learned peace, but your body has learned protection. Healing is the process of teaching your chest that peace is now safer than panic. Healing is training your physical self to trust what your spiritual self already knows. Healing is not the absence of physical symptoms, it is the integration of body and spirit until they agree that God is your refuge, not your emergency exit.

You are not failing. You are recalibrating. And God is patient with your process.

FAITH PRESCRIPTION

1. Speak this truth over your chest when it tightens: "Peace is my portion. My chest is reacting, but I am safe. God is here with me."

2. Place your hand on the center of your chest: Apply gentle pressure. Feel the warmth of your own touch. Say slowly: "Relax. Breathe. God is with us." Your nervous system responds to physical reassurance just as much as spiritual truth.

3. Declare these scriptures aloud:
- "My heart is steadfast, O God." (Psalm 57:7)
- "Let not your heart be troubled." (John 14:1)
- "The peace of God guards my heart and mind." (Philippians 4:7)

4. Engage grounding through breath: Inhale for 4 seconds. Exhale for 6 seconds. Tell your chest, "You are not in danger."

5. Limit catastrophic thoughts, increase compassion for your body. Your chest is reacting from old pain, not present danger. Treat it with kindness, not punishment.

HOLY SPIRIT CONSULT

The Holy Spirit does not shame your body for reacting. He does not roll His eyes at your chest tightening again. He does not dismiss your fear or minimize your symptoms. Instead, He draws near. He gently places peace where your tension is building. He speaks calmly into your sternum and steadiness into your heartbeat. He reminds you that He is not just the God of your spirit. He is God over your breathing, your pulse, your nervous system, and every emotional response that overwhelms you.

The Holy Spirit whispers: "Your chest is afraid, but I am not. Lean into My peace until your body learns from your spirit." He is patient with the parts of you that panic first. He is present in the moments when your breathing betrays your belief. He is compassionate toward the ache you cannot explain. And He is committed to healing the deeper root behind every tightening sensation. Your chest may preach fear, but the Holy Spirit is preaching peace louder.

GUIDED PRAYER

"Lord, You see the fear that rises in my chest before I even understand it. You see the pressure, the ache, the tightening, the alarms that go off for no reason. I bring it to You now. Calm my chest. Slow my heartbeat. Remind my body of the safety my spirit already knows. Help me breathe with You, not against You. Teach my chest to trust You the way my spirit does. Fill me with peace that overrides every false alarm. I invite You into the places where fear lives in my body. I trust You with every breath. Amen."

REFLECTION PAGE

*   What usually happens around me?

____

____

____

____

- What story does my chest tell me that my spirit knows isn't true?

____

____

____

- What memory could my body be responding to even when I'm unaware?

____

____

____

- How did God meet me the last time this happened?

____

____

- What would it look like to treat my body with the same compassion God treats me with?

____

____

____

____

____

____

____

____

____

DOCTOR'S ORDERS

✓ Your chest is reacting to history, not reality.

✓ You are safe, even when your chest disagrees.

✓ Practice breathing daily, not just in crisis.

✓ Don't argue with your chest, reassure it.

✓ Let Scripture speak louder than physical symptoms.

✓ Healing takes repetition, not perfection.

✓ God is with you in every heartbeat.

DR. PATRICIA S. TANNER

PERSONAL NOTES

34

Chapter 3:

Breathing? Never Heard Of It, The Spirited Battle With Hyperventilation

SYMPTOM: "My breath disappears the moment fear appears."

Hyperventilation is one of the most terrifying symptoms because it feels like your own body has turned against you. One moment you're breathing normally, minding your business, and the next moment your chest tightens, your breaths become shallow, and your lungs start acting like they were never properly trained for this job. You feel like you can't inhale enough oxygen. You feel like your throat is shrinking. You feel like the air is too thin. Your chest rises fast, your shoulders lift, your stomach goes still, and suddenly breathing, the one thing you've done effortlessly since birth, feels like a complicated exam you never studied for.

And the worst part? The panic feeds the breathlessness, and the breathlessness feeds the panic. Your body throws fuel on its own fire, and your mind becomes a frantic narrator: *"I can't breathe. What if I suffocate? What if this doesn't stop? What if I pass out? What if something is seriously wrong?"* Even though nothing life-threatening is happening, your lungs behave as if you're trapped under water. Your breath races ahead of logic, ahead of scripture, ahead of every calming thought you try to speak into your soul.

Then your spirit, small but steady, whispers, *"You've been here before. You made it before. You'll make it again. Breathe with Me."* But your body doesn't care. Your lungs are convinced this is a crisis. Your nervous system sounds like an internal alarm. Your breath becomes shallow, rapid, chaotic. You feel dizzy. Your fingers tingle. Your lips buzz. Your chest rises like you're sprinting, but you're sitting still.

This is the symptom: your breath abandoning you when fear arrives, leaving you feeling helpless, frightened, and certain you're running out of air even when oxygen is all around you. It feels like drowning in plain sight, with everyone else breathing easily while you struggle for every inhale.

TEACHING: Breath Is Both Biological and Spiritual, And Panic Targets Both

Breathing is the most sacred, foundational gift God ever gave you. Before you spoke, before you walked, before you cried your first tear, God breathed into you. Breath is not just air, it is life, divine design, and spiritual connection. So, when panic targets your breath, it's not just physical discomfort, it is a disruption of your sense of control, safety, and grounding. It feels like your connection to life itself is slipping away.

But hyperventilation is rarely about a lack of oxygen, it is almost always about **too much fear**. When panic rises, your body begins to breathe too fast, not too little. Your lungs overwork. Your chest expands more than necessary. You take in more oxygen than your body can use, and carbon dioxide drops too low. This imbalance creates the sensation of suffocation even though you are breathing *more* than enough. Hyperventilation is your body misinterpreting fear as danger and reacting with a survival-level response that doesn't match your reality.

Spiritually, this creates confusion. You're trying to breathe through a body that's convinced it's dying while your spirit is preaching peace you can't physically feel. You know God is with you, but your breathing patterns don't reflect that truth. You know  you're safe, but your lungs argue otherwise. And because breathing is so primal, so automatic, so essential, any disruption feels catastrophic.

But here is the truth panic never tells you: ***You have never stopped breathing.*** Your lungs have never actually failed you. Your breath has never abandoned you. Your brain is reacting to fear, not a lack of air. Your spirit is still intact beneath the waves of panic. Your breath has been with you through every episode, even the worst ones. And God? He has been in every inhale and every exhale, even the messy ones. Breath is not just a bodily function; it is a reminder of divine presence.

When God breathed into Adam, it wasn't a one-time event. That breath, *His breath*, became the pattern for every breath you take. Meaning: ***You breathe God in and out even when you don't feel Him.*** Your hyperventilation doesn't scare Him. Your shallow breath doesn't diminish Him. Your panic does not separate you from His presence. Healing comes when you learn to slow your body enough for your spirit to lead again, not in perfection, but in partnership. Your spirit knows peace. Your body can learn it.

FAITH PRESCRIPTION

1. Speak truth to your breath: "My lungs are safe. My breath is here. God breathed into me, and that breath has not left."

2. Practice rhythmic breathing: Inhale for 4 seconds Hold for 2 Exhale for 6 Repeat until your chest softens.

3. Place one hand on your stomach: Let your belly rise instead of your chest. Say, "This is peace entering my body."

4. Interrupt panic by grounding your senses: Name 5 things you see
4 things you can touch
3 sounds you hear

2 scents you smell
1 truth you know about God.

5. Keep a short Scripture by memory:
- "The breath of the Almighty gives me life." (Job 33:4)
- "In Him we live and move and have our being." (Acts 17:28)

HOLY SPIRIT CONSULT

The Holy Spirit is not distant from your breathlessness. He is the breath within it. He sits in the swirl of your hyperventilation and whispers steady truth: ***"You are not suffocating. You are not in danger. I am your breath. I am your stability. I am the calm you can't feel yet."*** He slows your breath not by force but by presence. He fills the tight spaces with assurance. He surrounds your lungs with peace that reaches farther than fear. He reminds you that He hovered over chaos in Genesis, and He hovers over the chaos inside your chest now. The Holy Spirit is patient with every shaky inhale. He is kind to every shallow exhale. And He restores your breathing, not instantly, but faithfully.

GUIDED PRAYER

"Holy Spirit, I bring You my breath, the fast ones, the shallow ones, the shaky ones. You see how fear grips my lungs and steals my calm. Help me breathe with You, not against You. Slow my body where it feels rushed. Quiet my mind where it feels overwhelmed. Remember that I am not losing air. I am losing fear. Teach my lungs the rhythm of peace. Let every breath I take be evidence that You are with me. Inhale Your truth. Exhale every lie. Amen."

REFLECTION PAGE

- What does hyperventilation feel like in my body?

____

____

____

____

- What thoughts usually follow my breathlessness?

____

____

____

____

- What lies does fear tell me during panic?

____

____

____

____

- What truth do I want to replace it with?

____

____

____

____

- How did God meet me in my breathing today?

____

____

____

____

____

____

____

____

DOCTOR'S ORDERS

✓ Slow breathing is spiritual warfare, practice it daily.

✓ Keep your shoulders lowered when panic rises.

✓ Your lungs have never failed you, remind yourself of that.

✓ Never breathe through panic alone; let your spirit partner with your breath.

✓ Fear exaggerates sensations, truth stabilizes them.

✓ Talk to your body kindly; it listens to your tone.

✓ You are safe. You are breathing. You will get through this.

DR. PATRICIA S. TANNER

PERSONAL NOTES

42

Chapter 4:

Palpitations, Sweaty Palms, And The Lies Your Brain Believes At 2:00 A.M.

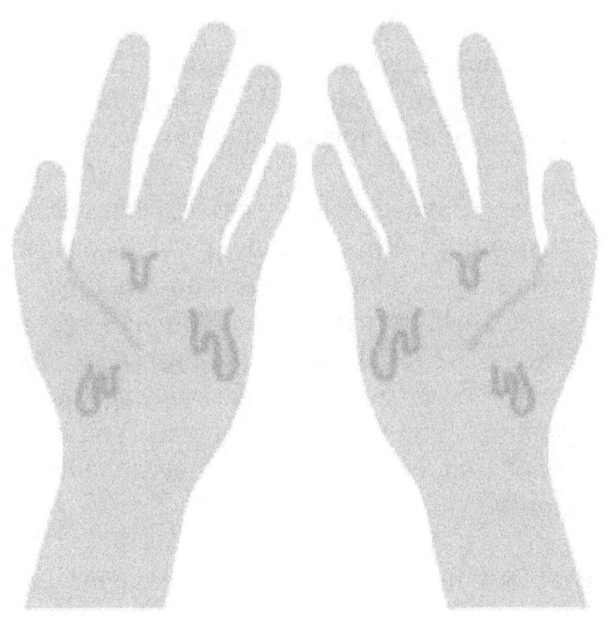

SYMPTOM: "Everything feels worse at night, especially my thoughts."

There is a specific kind of panic that wakes up with the moon. It doesn't matter how peaceful your day was or how well things were going, nighttime panic has its own personality. The sun goes down, the house gets quiet, the distractions fade, and suddenly your body starts rehearsing every symptom it's ever had. Your heart beats louder. Your breathing feels too shallow. Your chest feels tight. Your mind becomes a loudspeaker for every worst-case scenario it can invent.

During the day, your logic has friends, noise, people, light, movement, tasks. At night, logic is outnumbered. Darkness amplifies fear. Silence exaggerates symptoms. Stillness gives every anxious thought a front-row seat. And your body? It decides to hold a full spiritual-physical conference without your consent.

Your palms begin to sweat. Your heartbeat feels irregular. Your breath gets inconsistent. Your muscles are tense. Your stomach flips. Your mind starts whispering lies like: *"Something is wrong with you." "This is the night everything falls apart." "You're not going to make it through this episode." " You need help, now."* You know it's irrational. You know it's fear. You know it's not God, but your brain believes the darkness gives fear more authority.

This is the symptom: nighttime turning into a magnifying glass that enlarges every fear, every sensation, and every lie your anxiety tries to preach. You feel weaker at night because you are more vulnerable, not spiritually, but physically. My body is tired. The emotions are unfiltered. The mind wants answers it's too exhausting to process. And the enemy knows exhaustion is fertile ground for deception.

Nothing is worse than lying in bed at 2 A.M. with a heart that won't calm down and a mind that won't shut up. It feels like a private war, and the hardest part is that no one else sees it but you.

TEACHING: Night Is Not More Dangerous, It Just Feels Louder

There is nothing spiritually inferior about you because anxiety hits harder at night. Night has always been the time when the human mind wrestles more intensely. Even David wrote, *"I flood my bed with tears."* People don't usually spiral at noon. Spiral season shows up when distractions disappear.

Here's the truth: Your symptoms do not get worse at night, your awareness does. During the day, noise protects you. Conversations distract you. Activity grounds you. Movement keeps your mind occupied. But when the world quiets down, your mind finally has space to speak   and because it has not been taught how to process fear in stillness, it panics.

Night also pulls up old memories. The mind stores unresolved fear in silence. The nervous system becomes more alert when there are fewer stimuli to focus on. Your brain misreads the calm as danger. Your body misreads the quiet as threat. Your emotions misread solitude as vulnerability. And darkness becomes a stage for every unresolved fear to perform.

But here is spiritual truth: The God who watches you during the day keeps the same strength during the night. Fear doesn't grow in the dark, it just becomes more noticeable. God doesn't shrink in the dark, you just feel more exposed. Nighttime is not the enemy. Nighttime is where healing happens. Nighttime is where truth is proven. Nighttime is where faith becomes less about feelings and more about foundation. It is in the middle of the night that your spirit whispers, "We're okay. God has not gone anywhere. This is fear, not prophecy. This is sensation, not danger."

Your brain may believe lies at 2 A.M. but your spirit tells the truth even then. God does not lose track of you when the lights go out. Your chest is not more vulnerable. Your breath is not more fragile. Your body is not more threatened. Fear is just louder because the world is quieter.

FAITH PRESCRIPTION

1. Speak this as soon as nighttime fear rises: "This darkness is no danger. God is here in the night just like He is in the day."

2. Put your hand on your heart: Feel your heartbeat. Say slowly: "Calm down. We are safe. We are not under attack."

3. Use a nighttime scripture:
- "I lay down and sleep; I wake again, because the Lord sustains me." (Psalm 3:5)
- "He gives His beloved sleep." (Psalm 127:2)

4. Ground your body: Relax your shoulders. Unclench your jaw . Loosen your stomach. Releasing your hands. Let your body feel the bed beneath you.

5. Interrupt spirals with gratitude:
List three things God did today, even small ones. This shifts the brain from survival to stability.

HOLY SPIRIT CONSULT

The Holy Spirit does not sleep, and He does not leave when it gets dark. He stands guard over you while you lie in bed trembling. He watches every breath, every heartbeat, every thought. He whispers truth into the lies your brain believes at 2 A.M. He reassures you: "Nothing is happening. Nothing is wrong with you. This is fear pretending to be prophecy. I am here in the stillness. I am here in the shaking. Rest in Me." The Holy Spirit is the One who turns midnight panic into midnight peace, not by changing the night, but by calming the storm inside of you.

GUIDED PRAYER

"God, The night feels louder than the day. My thoughts run faster, my heart beats harder, and fear grows bigger when everything else gets quiet. But I know You are here. You are not intimidated by my nighttime panic. You are not absent from my midnight anxiety. Calm my mind. Quite lies. Protect my body from fear that pretends to be truth. Let Your presence fills my room, my chest, my thoughts, and my breath. Help me sleep in the safety of Your presence. I trust You with my night. Amen."

REFLECTION PAGE

- What tends to trigger my nighttime spirals?

____

____

____

- What lies do I tend to believe most at night?

- How does my body respond differently in the dark?

- What scriptures bring me the most comfort when I can't sleep?

- What does my spirit whisper when fear gets loud?

____

____

____

____

____

____

____

____

____

____

DOCTOR'S ORDERS

✓ Nighttime fear is common, not catastrophic.

✓ Fear feels louder in silence, but it is not more powerful.

✓ Keep a calming scripture ready before bed.

✓ Relax your body, fear can't stay where the body is at rest.

✓ Do not fight the night, invite God into it.

✓ You've survived every midnight before; you'll survive this one too.

✓ You are safe in the dark because God is still awake.

DR. PATRICIA S. TANNER

PERSONAL NOTES

50

Chapter 5:

"You Said You Wanted Freedom, But You Still Want Control"

SYMPTOM: Wanting God's Promises Without God's Process

 You ever pray one of those dangerous prayers like, *"Lord, have Your way,"* and then immediately regret it when He does? You wanted peace, and He sent pruning. You asked for direction, and He sent delays. You begged for clarity, and He gave you… conviction. Now you're sitting there, clutching your planner and your pride, whispering, *"This is not what I meant."*

Welcome to the control issue most believers don't want to talk about, the one where you say "Yes, Lord" but secretly hope He consults your preferences first. You love the idea of freedom, but you hate the part where it means letting go of the steering wheel. You say, "God, take over," but you keep one hand on the gearshift, just in case.

The symptom shows up like this:
- You're frustrated when plans change but call it "discernment."
- You overthink everything God already settled.
- You trust God's will, until it interrupts your comfort.
- You quote Jeremiah 29:11, but you're quietly editing verse 11b to include *your* timeline.

You want control, not because you don't love God, but because you don't *like* uncertainty. Control gives you the illusion of peace; the same way a security blanket gives a child comfort during a storm. The problem is it doesn't stop the rain.

And here's the irony: the tighter you hold on, the more things slip through your fingers. You're exhausted, not because God isn't working, but because you won't stop trying to work *for* Him. You're so busy managing outcomes that you've forgotten the One who manages the universe. You say you want freedom, but the only thing you refuse to free is your grip.

TEACHING: The Biblical Pattern of Surrender

Let's be honest: surrendering is terrifying. It sounds poetic in worship songs, but it feels painful in real life. Because real surrender means relinquishing control over how things unfold, even when you don't understand the "why."

The Bible is full of people who learned the hard way that freedom requires surrender:

- **Abraham** had to give up Isaac, not because God wanted his son, but because God wanted his *trust.*
- **Moses** had to give up his stuttering excuses and walk back into Egypt, the place of his greatest failure.
- **Mary** had to give up her reputation to say yes to an assignment that would change the world.
- And **Jesus**, the ultimate example, gave up His will in the garden and said, *"Not my will, but Yours be done."*

That last one? That's where real freedom lives.

Here's the paradox: control and peace cannot coexist. You can't experience divine rest while fighting divine order. You can't walk in freedom while trying to edit God's instructions. Every miracle, 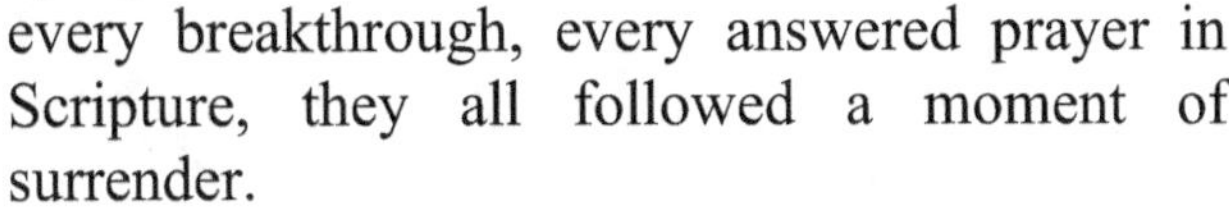 every breakthrough, every answered prayer in Scripture, they all followed a moment of surrender.

Think about it: the Red Sea didn't part until Moses *stopped panicking* and *lifted his staff.* The oil didn't multiply until the widow *started pouring.* The walls of Jericho didn't fall until the people *stopped questioning and started marching.*

Surrender isn't losing control; it's *giving control to the only One who can handle it.* But your flesh hates that, doesn't it? Because surrender feels powerless. You want proof before obedience, clarity before commitment, and control before comfort. But faith doesn't work like that. Faith says, "I'll follow before I understand." When you say, "God, I got this," you're operating in pride. When you say, "God, You've got this," you're operating in faith. One keeps you busy; the other keeps you balanced.

Here's the truth that might sting a little: *you can't be both the driver and the passenger in your destiny.* If you keep trying to control everything, you'll never learn what it means to *trust* anything. God isn't asking you to stop caring. He's asking you to stop carrying. Because freedom isn't found in the absence of structure; it's found in the surrender of self. And the moment you finally launch your fists; you'll discover that what you were gripping so tightly wasn't security, it was stressful.

FAITH PRESCRIPTION

Medication: *Luke 22:42 (NIV) "Father, if You are willing, take this cup from Me; yet not My will, but Yours be done."*
Dosage:
- Take every morning before making any life-altering decisions.
- Swallow whole. do not chew or overanalyze.
- Works best when paired with deep breaths, worship, and waiting.

Warning Label: May cause temporary discomfort followed by permanent peace. Side effects include clarity, joy, and realizing God's plan was better all along.

HOLY SPIRIT CONSULT

You keep praying for peace while gripping control, and the Holy Spirit keeps whispering: *"You can't have both."* He's not trying to take things *from* you. He's trying to give things *to* you. But your hands are too full of your own plans to receive them. When you start losing control, don't panic, that's usually when the Holy Spirit is doing His best work. He specializes in disrupting comfort to develop character. He'll gently remind you, *"You said you wanted freedom, remember?"* And when you nod, tired and humbled, He'll add, *"Then let Me lead."*

The Holy Spirit doesn't force surrender, He invites it. He knows your tendency to overthink. He knows your fear of the unknown. But He also knows what's waiting on the other side of your obedience: rest, direction, and results you couldn't produce in a lifetime of striving. So, the next time He nudges you to let go, don't fight Him, follow Him. You'll never experience divine control while clinging to human comfort.

GUIDED PRAYER

Lord, I confess that I love control more than I admit. I've prayed for freedom while still demanding the driver's seat. I've called my plans "faith," when really, they were fear in disguise. Today, I surrendered, again. Even the parts I don't understand. Even the things I thought I needed to manage. I lay down my timelines, my expectations, my backup plans, and my pride. You are God, and I am not. Teach me to rest in Your control, not wrestle with it. I trust that Your will is better than my way. In Jesus' Name, Amen.

REFLECTION PAGE + JOURNAL PROMPTS

Self-Check: When do you feel the most anxious, when you're trusting God or when you're trying to manage Him?

____

____

____

JOURNAL PROMPTS:

1. What situation am I trying to control right now that's draining my peace?

____

____

____

____

2. Why does surrender feel like losing power to me?

____

____

____

____

3. When has God proven that His way worked better than mine?

4. What would my life look like if I trusted God completely for one full week, no interference, no backup plan?

Takeaway Reminder: Control is a counterfeit version of comfort. Freedom isn't about holding on tighter; it's about trusting deeper. The safest place you'll ever be is out of your own hands and inside His will.

PERSONAL NOTES

58

Chapter 6:
YOUR NERVOUS SYSTEM ISN'T SAVED

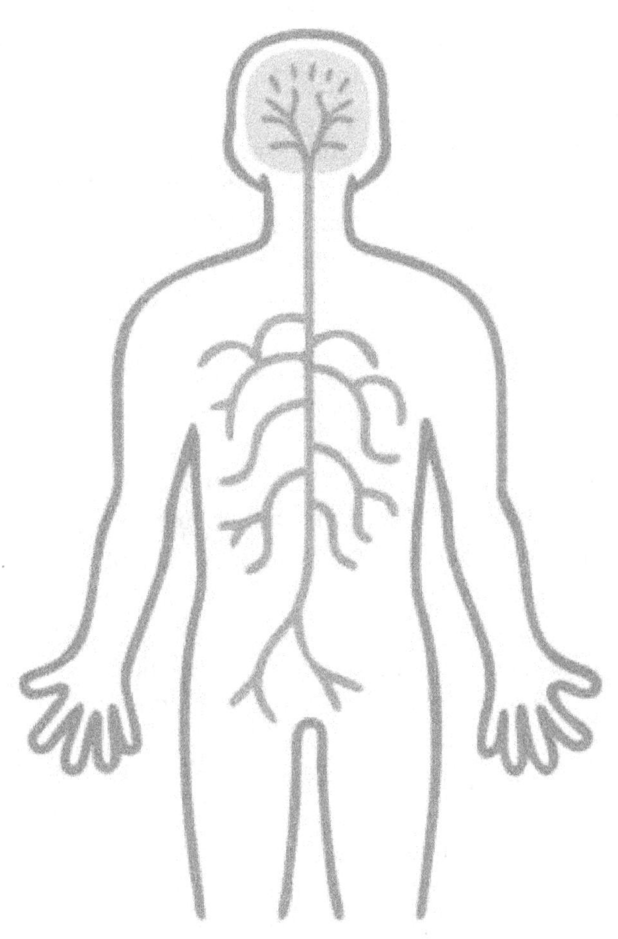

SYMPTOM: "Why does my body react like I'm dying when my spirit knows better?"

There is a moment every believer battling anxiety knows too well, the moment when your body acts like it never meets your spirit. You're sitting there, fully aware of God's presence, fully trusting that He's with you, fully believing the truth you've been taught… and suddenly your nervous system hits the panic switch like you're being chased by lions in the Old Testament.

Your heart pounds like it's sending an SOS signal. Your breath shortens like oxygen is being rationed. Your chest tightens like pressure is pressing in from every side. Your muscles brace as if preparing for impact. Your throat feels tight, your stomach flips, and your hands tremble as if your spirit forgot to brief the rest of your body on today's itinerary.

Nothing triggered it. Nothing justified it. Nothing warranted such a dramatic response. Yet your body behaves as if danger is licking the back of your neck. The frustration is real, because you know God. You know peace. You know the enemy is defeated. You know your life is not in danger. Yet your body insists on throwing a physiological tantrum that contradicts everything your spirit believes. You start wondering: "Is this spiritual warfare?" "Is this a sign?" "Is this me losing control?" "Is God disappointed that I feel this way?" But deep down, you also feel this: "I shouldn't be responding like this… not after all God has done for me."

This is the symptom: your nervous system reacting out of instinct, not revelation, choosing fear even when your spirit has chosen faith. It feels like betrayal. It feels like weakness. It feels like something is wrong with you. But none of those things are true. Your nervous system isn't saved, but God still uses it.

TEACHING: Your Nervous System Learns Through Experience, Your Spirit Learns Through Truth

Your nervous system has one job: survival. It doesn't care about theology, trust, or spiritual growth. It responds to fear, memory, trauma, and perceived threats even when the threat no longer exists. Your spirit, however, responds to truth, revelation, and the presence of God. Your spirit knows peace. Your spirit knows safety.

Your spirit knows the sound of God's voice saying, "Fear not." The problem isn't that your spirit is weak. It's that your body hasn't caught up yet. Your nervous system was shaped by experiences long before your spirit matured. It remembers every betrayal. It remembers every threat. It remembers every moment of abandonment. It reminds me of every unsafe environment. And because it remembers, it reacts, sometimes violently, sometimes irrationally, sometimes without warning.

You can be spiritually strong and physically overwhelmed at the same time. You can trust God deeply and still have a nervous system running old survival algorithms. That's not spiritual failure, that's physiology. But here is the hope: Your nervous system can be retrained. Your body can learn what your spirit already knows. Your biology can come into alignment with your belief. God does not shame your body. He designed it. He understands its signals, its alarms, its overreactions. He is patient with you while your nervous system relearns safety.

You are not spiritually defective because your body panics. You are not less anointed because your hands shake. You are not a weak believer because your heart races. You are a human walking through the sacred process of rewiring your inner world with God's help. Healing is not instant. Alignment takes time. But God is committed to both your spirit and your nervous system, and He will bring them into harmony.

FAITH PRESCRIPTION

1. Speak this truth when your body overreacts: "My nervous system is reacting, but I am safe. My spirit knows the truth, and my body will catch up."

2. Practice body-spirit alignment: Place one hand on your heart. Place the other on your stomach. Say: "Heart, be still. Breath, slow down. Spirit, lead."

3. Declare scripture that speaks to both body and spirit:
- "Be still and know that I am God." (Psalm 46:10)
- "My flesh and my heart may fail, but God is the strength of my heart." (Psalm 73:26)
- "Peace I leave with you; My peace I give you." (John 14:27)

4. Engage your senses: Look at something stable. Touch something solid. Breathe in something calming. Sit in the presence of something familiar.

5. Remind yourself gently: "This is biology, not prophecy."

HOLY SPIRIT CONSULT

The Holy Spirit does not shame your nervous system. He understands the alarms it sounds, the signals it sends, and the fear it holds onto. He stands beside you, inside you, around you, and whispers truth into every trembling cell: "Your body is not your enemy. I will teach it peace. I will calm down what is overwhelmed. I will soothe what is afraid. I will align what feels divided." He brings order into the places where your body feels chaotic. He brings comfort into the places where your heart feels threatened. He brings grounding into the places where your breath feels unstable. And He assures you that He is Lord over your nervous system too, every neuron, every impulse, every sensation. He does not wait for your body to be calm before He shows up. He shows up *to* calm your body.

GUIDED PRAYER

"Holy Spirit, My nervous system reacts faster than my faith sometimes. My body panics even when my spirit is at peace. But I bring both to You, the calm and the chaos. Teach my body the truth my spirit already knows. Steady my heart. Slow my breath. Silence the alarms that misinterpret fear as danger. Align my biology with Your peace. Thank You for being gentle with my humanity and patient with my healing. Amen."

REFLECTION PAGE

- When does my nervous system overreact the most?

____

____

____

____

____

- What physical sensations do I fear the most, and why?

____

____

- What truth does my spirit know that my body hasn't fully learned?

- What would it look like to offer God my physical symptoms without shame?

- How has God shown up for me even in the middle of panic?

____

____

____

____

____

____

____

____

____

DOCTOR'S ORDERS

✓ You are not broken, you are rewiring.

✓ Your body reacts based on memory, not truth.

✓ Patience is a spiritual discipline when healing your nervous system.

✓ Practice grounding daily, not just in panic moments.

✓ Keep aligning your breath with your beliefs.

✓ God is restoring both your spirit and your biology.

✓ Healing is happening, even if your body hasn't felt it yet.

DR. PATRICIA S. TANNER

PERSONAL NOTES

Chapter 7:

FIGHT-OR-FLIGHT: THE DRAMA QUEEN LIVING IN YOUR RIBCAGE

SYMPTOM: "My body jumps to conclusions my spirit never agreed to."

There is a moment in anxiety where your body seems to shout, "EVERYBODY PANIC!" while absolutely nothing is happening. It is a jumpy feeling. The sudden jolt. The instant rush of adrenaline. The urge to run, hide, escape, or collapse, all in under three seconds. It's when someone drops a spoon in the kitchen and your entire soul asks, "Is this how I die?" It's when your chest tightens at the smallest sound, your shoulders shoot up around your ears, and your heart acts like it's auditioning for an action movie scene you didn't consent to.

Fight-or-flight is dramatic. Loud. Reactive. Overprotective.

And slightly disrespectful, if we're being honest. It hijacks your body like a bad driver with too much caffeine. Your muscles stiffen. Your stomach clenches. Your eyes widen. Your hands get sweaty. Your pulse spikes. Your thoughts sprint like someone hit fast-forward. And yet, your spirit is fine. Calm. Centered. Aware of God. Anchored in truth.

This is the symptom: your fight-or-flight system firing false alarms, dragging your body into emergency mode even when your spirit is at rest. It's not danger. It's not prophecy. It's not a sign. It's simply your internal survival switch stuck on "high." And it's exhausting, because you're living a peaceful life with a body that acts like the world is a battlefield.

TEACHING: Fight-Or-Flight Is Not A Demon, It Is A System God Created That Life Damaged

Fight-or-flight is part of your God-designed biology. He created it to protect you from actual danger, lions, cliffs, thieves, car crashes, real emergencies. But trauma, stress, exhaustion, fear conditioning, and chronic anxiety trained your fight-or-flight to respond to things that aren't dangerous at all.

Your nervous system isn't sinful. It's scary. It's doing too much because life has done too much to you. Here's what most believers misunderstand: **your** fight-or-flight system cannot tell the difference between a real threat and a remembered one. So, when something reminds your body, even subconsciously, of a past wound, disappointment, or fear, your biology reacts as if it's happening again.

This doesn't mean you're weak. It means you're human. It means you've lived. It means you've survived. And surviving leaves mark. Spiritually, this creates tension, because your spirit is learning trust while your body is still learning safety. Your spirit knows God is faithful. Your spirit remembers the miracles. Your spirit believes His promises. But your body? It reminds me of the pain. The panic. The abandonment. The fear. The betrayal. The helplessness. And when those memories fire, even silently, fight-or-flight launches.

But here's the truth, your body needs time to learn: You don't live there anymore. You're not in danger anymore. You are not who you were when those wounds were formed. And the God you trust is bringing your biology into alignment with your belief. God does not punish you for having a reactive nervous system. He heals you through it, layer by layer, episode by episode, breath by breath. He is retraining your fight-or-flight to stop panicking in the shadows. Your spirit is already growing in truth. Your body is simply learning that truth more slowly. And God is patient with both.

FAITH PRESCRIPTION

1. Speak this over your body: "My fight-or-flight is activated, but I am safe. God is here. My body will learn peace."

2. Interrupt the adrenaline cycle: Sit down or place both feet flat on the ground. Relax your shoulders. Unclench your jaw. Loosen your hands. Tell your body: "Stand down. This is not an emergency."

3. Declare scriptures that calm the survival system:
- "The Lord is my refuge and strength." (Psalm 46:1)
- "I will fear no evil, for You are with me." (Psalm 23:4)
- "In peace I will lie down and sleep." (Psalm 4:8)

4. Activate the parasympathetic system: Long slow exhale Repeat And repeat again Your exhale tells your fight-or-flight system that the battle is over.

5. Reduce body-blame: Your body is not your enemy; it is doing its best with old information.

HOLY SPIRIT CONSULT

The Holy Spirit meets you in the moment your body overreacts. He does not shame your adrenaline. He does not rebuke your trembling. He does not demand that your biology instantly match your theology. Instead, He places peace under your ribs, the very place where fear tries to rise. He whispers: "You are not in danger. I am with you. I hold your heartbeat. I calm your alarms. I lead your body into the safety your spirit already knows." He is patient with your survival instincts. He understands why they fire. He knows what hurts you. He knows what shaped you. And He knows exactly how to heal you. The Holy Spirit is not asking you to silence your fight-or-flight; He is teaching it how to rest.

GUIDED PRAYER

"Holy Spirit, My body reacts faster than my mind and louder than my spirit. My adrenaline rises even when nothing is wrong. But I

give my fight-or-flight system to You. Calm the alarms that misread fear as danger. Quiet reactions that do not match my reality. Steady my breath, my chest, my heart, and my thoughts. Teach my body the safety that my spirit already trusts. Thank You for being gentle with me. Amen."

REFLECTION PAGE

- What situations trigger my fight-or-flight the most?

____

____

- What physical sensations scare me the quickest?

____

____

____

- What truths does my spirit know that my body still doubts?

____

____

- How has God shown me safety in seasons when fear used to rule me?

____

____

- What does emotional safety feel like inside my body?

DOCTOR'S ORDERS

✓ Your fight-or-flight system is confused, not cursed.

✓ Your body needs reassurance, not rebuke.

✓ Breathe slowly, your exhale is your weapon.

✓ Practice grounding before panic begins.

✓ Trust that God is healing your reactions, not judging them.

✓ Your spirit leads; your body follows, give it time.

✓ You are safe. You are covered. You are learning peace.

Chapter 8:

TRAUMA TRIGGERS THAT DON'T CARE ABOUT YOUR SCRIPTURE MEMORY

SYMPTOM: "I thought I healed from that... so why does my body still react?"

There is a unique frustration that comes when your body responds to something long after your mind believes it has moved on. You'll be living your life, fully functional, spiritually stable, emotionally grounded, and then something small happens. A sound. A scent. A tone of voice. A facial expression. A location. A memory. A sudden shift in atmosphere. Something so subtle that another person would never notice. But your body notices. And before you can even name what's happening, your chest tightens, your breath shallows, your stomach drops, and your nerves light up like flashing warning signs. You freeze. You panic. You dissociate. You shut down. You go numb. You overthink. You react like you're reliving something you thought you buried years ago.

And the worst part is that it feels irrational. You're not in danger. You're not in the past. You're not facing the person who hurt you. You're not experiencing the same trauma. But your body doesn't know that. Your body responds to familiar sensations, not healed conclusions.

The trigger doesn't ask permission. It doesn't ask if you prayed this morning. It doesn't ask how many scriptures you memorized. It doesn't ask how much spiritual growth you've had. It doesn't matter that you forgave them. It doesn't matter that you processed it. It doesn't matter that you're living a new life. Your body reacts like the old wound is still open, even when your spirit knows God has brought you far from that pain.

This is the symptom: your nervous system responding to a trigger faster than your conscious mind can process it, making you feel like your healing is defective, when your body is still catching up to the freedom your spirit has embraced.

TEACHING: Your Spirit Moves On Instantly, Your Body Moves On Gradually

Trauma is stored differently from other memories. It doesn't file neatly away in your brain. It stays wired into your nervous system. Meaning your body remembers what your spirit has already released.

You may have been spiritually forgiven. You may have emotionally processed. You may have mentally understood. But your body? It stored the physical sensations of that fear. And the body holds onto sensation longer than the spirit holds onto story. That is why a raised voice that isn't threatening can still make your chest throb. That is why a certain smell can bring back memories you haven't thought of in years. That is why a room, a date, a situation, or a person who resembles someone from your past can activate fear faster than you can pray.

Your triggers do not mean you're not healed. Your triggers mean you had experiences intense enough that your body did what God designed it to do: *protect you.* But now that you're safe, that same protection becomes overreaction. Spiritually, you may have moved on. But biologically, you must retrain your body to stop mistaking the present for the past.

Think of it like this: Your spirit received the revelation. Your mind accepted the truth. Your body is still buffering. And God is patient with buffering. Healing from trauma is not a sign of spiritual immaturity, it is proof that you are human and in need of God's gentle rewiring. The goal is not to eliminate

triggers overnight. The goal is to become so anchored in God's presence that the trigger loses its power.

God does not rush you. He walks with you through each layer.

He heals what you didn't even realize was still alive in your body. He touches the memories you never verbalized. He soothes the sensations you've been afraid to name. Your trauma triggers do not disqualify your healing; they highlight where God is still lovingly working.

FAITH PRESCRIPTION

1. Name the trigger without judging yourself: "My body reacted, but I am safe. This is a trigger, not a threat."

2. Use grounding + truth together: Grounding: touch something solid (chair, floor, clothing). Truth: "I am in the present. The past cannot touch me here."

3. Speak Scripture that reconnects spirit + body:
- "He restores my soul." (Psalm 23:3)
- "Perfect love casts out fear." (1 John 4:18)
- "The Lord is close to the brokenhearted." (Psalm 34:18)

4. Slow your breathing: Inhale: "I am safe." Exhale: "God is here." Repeat until your chest softens.

5. Do not shame your body, comfort it. Say, "Thank you for trying to protect me. But we are safe now."

HOLY SPIRIT CONSULT

The Holy Spirit understands your trauma triggers better than you do. He knows the memories you buried. He knows the sensations that shaped you. He knows the nights you didn't speak about. He knows the moments your heart fractured. And He does not pressure you when your body remembers what you wish it would forget. He enters the trigger with you saying: "I am here. You are not back there. You are not in danger. I am in your present, and I am healing the echoes of your past." He stands between you and the memory. He covers the place where fear rises. He whispers peace into the places where panic tries to live. He comforts your nervous system with the gentleness of a Father who knows your story in full. Your triggers do not intimidate the Holy Spirit. He uses them as doorways for deeper healing.

GUIDED PRAYER

"Holy Spirit, My body remembers things my mind has moved on from. Triggers rise without warning, and fear follows fast. But I invite You into these reactions. Heal the parts of me that still feel unsafe. Calm memories stored in my body. Cover the places where trauma left its fingerprints. Teach my nervous system the truth my spirit already knows that I am safe, loved, protected, and held. Walk me through every trigger until fear loses its power. Amen."

REFLECTION PAGE

- What situations or sensations tend to trigger me the most?

____

____

____

____

____

____

- How does my body react before my mind identifies the trigger?

____

____

____

____

____

- What lies does fear tell me in those moments?

____

____

____

- What truth does God speak over me instead?

____

____

____

- How has God shown up in past triggers I survived?

____

____

____

____

____

____

____

____

____

____

____

DOCTOR'S ORDERS

✓ Triggers are memories, not prophecies.

✓ Your body is reacting from old pain, not current danger.

✓ Ground yourself before you interpret sensations.

✓ Sit with the Holy Spirit in the trigger, don't run from it.

✓ Celebrate small victories; healing is layered.

✓ Never shame your body for remembering.

✓ You are in the present, and God is here with you.

DR. PATRICIA S. TANNER

PERSONAL NOTES

Chapter 9:

WHY YOUR SPIRIT TRUSTS GOD BUT YOUR BODY NEVER GOT THE MEMO

SYMPTOM: "I trust God with all my heart, so why is my body still panicking like I don't?"

There is an internal conflict that almost no one talks about because it feels embarrassing, confusing, and spiritually contradictory. It is the moment when your faith is strong, your relationship with God is secure, your prayer life is active, and your trust in Him is genuine, yet your body continues to react like it has absolutely no idea that you have matured spiritually.

You can stand in church with your hands lifted high, fully aware of God's presence surrounding you like a warm blanket, deeply moved by His goodness and overwhelmed by His love, and still feel your chest tightening in discomfort, your stomach knotting itself into anxiety loops, and your heart pounding as if it is preparing for a crisis that does not exist in reality. You may know without question that God is faithful and that He has carried you through storms much larger than anything you are facing now, yet your body misinterprets ordinary stress as catastrophic danger.

You can have a deep, unwavering trust in God and still experience trembling hands, jumpy nerves, and muscles that stiffen without your permission. You may speak scripture with absolute conviction, knowing that God has never failed you, yet your lungs behave as if they forgot how to expand fully, leaving you feeling breathless even in the safest environments. You may rest in God's promises, meditate on His Word, recall His past miracles, and still have your mind attempt to spiral into worry because your nervous system is convinced something terrible is about to happen. You notice a painful split happening inside yourself: one part of you is calm, confident, assured, peaceful, and spiritually grounded, while the other part is jittery, unsettled, tense, and preparing for impact.

This contradiction can make you feel defective, as if you are living a double life inside one body. You find yourself wondering if you are doing something wrong spiritually or if you missed a step in your healing journey. You question why your faith does not automatically override your symptoms. You wonder why your trust in God does not silence the alarms in your chest. You may even feel guilty, as if your physical reactions reflect spiritual weakness. And the disappointment grows when other Christians, who mean well but know very little about anxiety, say things like "Just trust God," "Stop worrying," "You should pay more," or "It's all in your mind," as if your nervous system is something you can switch off with a Bible verse.

But the truth, the truth you have never been told enough, is that your body and your spirit operate on two entirely different systems, and they do not always communicate well with one another. Your spirit responds to truth, revelation, and the presence of God, while your body responds to patterns, memory, fear, and survival instincts formed long before your spiritual maturity caught up. Your spirit can feel safe while your body still feels threatened. You can know you are protected while your chest feels vulnerable. You can believe

God wholeheartedly while your nervous system behaves like you are in danger. This is not hypocrisy. It is not a lack of devotion. It is not a failure of faith. It is simply the physical manifestation of emotional wounds that your spirit has moved on from, but your body has not fully unlearned yet.

This symptom is deeply frustrating because it feels like you are walking through life with two different realities operating inside of you. You feel betrayed by your own body, which seems determined to keep you in a state of vigilance even though your spirit has found rest. You want to scream, "Why am I still reacting like this? I know the truth now!" You feel irritated that your faith is strong but your biology has not yet caught up. And you feel exhausted navigating a version of yourself that loves God deeply while still being startled by shadows your spirit no longer fears.

This disconnect is real, painful, and often misunderstood. Yet it is one of the most common experiences among believers who have suffered trauma, endured chronic stress, or lived through seasons where fear shaped their physical responses even after God healed their spiritual identity. You are not alone in this battle between your spirit and your nervous system; you are simply in a stage of healing where your body is still catching up to the freedom your spirit already knows.

TEACHING: Your Spirit Learned God, Your Body Learned Survival. And Healing Is Teaching Them To Walk Together.

Your spirit and your body do not grow at the same pace, and they certainly do not learn the same lessons in the same way. Your spirit learns through revelation, prayer, encounter, worship, and the voice of God speaking into the deepest parts of your identity. It grows the moment you hear truth. It strengthens the moment you trust. It stabilizes the moment you surrender. Your spirit can shift instantly when God speaks, even if your emotions and physical responses do not shift with it. That is the beauty of faith: your inner man can believe what your outer man has not yet learned how to feel.

Your body, however, does not learn through revelation. It is learnt through repetition. It is taught through history. It learns through memories stored in muscle tension, breathing patterns, and survival responses that formed long before your spiritual awakening. Your spirit experiences God's presence and finds rest, but your body remembers the nights you cried yourself to sleep, the seasons you were emotionally abandoned, the times danger was real, and the moments fear shaped your responses. Your body learned to react fast because there were periods of your life were reacting fast kept you alive emotionally, mentally, or physically. Your nervous system was trained to overprotect you, and now that you are safe, it still behaves as if the world is unsafe.

Your spirit learns truth. Your body learns instincts. Your spirit trusts God's protection. Your body trusts your past pain. Your spirit receives peace as revelation. Your body must practice peace repeatedly to feel it.

When you encounter God, your spirit says, "We are safe now." But your body says, "Prove it." When you pray, your spirit says, "God is here." But your body says, "We've been alone before, I need time to trust this." When you declare scripture, your spirit says, "It is finished." But your body says, "It may be finished spiritually, but I still feel the residue." This is not spiritual immaturity; it is physiological memory. Your nervous system can store fear even after your heart has learned freedom. Your body can retain patterns even after your spirit has embraced peace.

God does not get offended that your body has not caught up to your spirit. He understands human design better than you ever could. He knows that trauma shapes the body differently than it shapes the soul. He knows that trust takes time to settle into your biology. He knows that healing happens in layers, not leaps. And He is  incredibly patient with every part of you, not just the parts that feel holy.

The journey of healing is not just your spirit trusting God; it is your body learning that it can trust God too. Your body needs consistency, gentleness, compassion, and patience. It needs repetition of calm moments. It needs to experience safety repeatedly before it stops reacting to old patterns. It needs to learn what your spirit already knows that God is not just a protector of your soul, but a protector of your entire being.

Healing is when your body begins to respond to peace the same way it used to respond to fear. Healing is when your spirit's confidence begins to seep into your breath, your heartbeat, your muscles, and your nervous system. Healing is when your biology finally aligns with your belief. This does not happen overnight. It happens through intentional partnership with God, compassionate self-awareness, repetitive grounding, and a refusal to shame yourself for having a human response to past pain.

Your body is not behind. Your body is not rebellious. Your body is not spiritually disconnected. Your body is healing, slowly, beautifully, faithfully, and God is walking with you through every tremor, every false alarm, every spike of fear, and every moment of dysregulation.

You are not spiritually failing. You are spiritually leading your body into the wholeness God already promised. And one day, your body will respond with peace as naturally as it once responded with panic.

FAITH PRESCRIPTION

Helping Your Body Learn What Your Spirit Already Believes

Your healing in this chapter begins with the understanding that your body is not stubborn, rebellious, or spiritually resistant; it is simply conditioned by experiences that taught it to react before thinking. The goal of this prescription is to help your body slowly begin to trust the peace your spirit already knows. One of the most powerful ways to start this process is to express alignment over yourself, not as a command but as a compassionate invitation. You will place your hand over your chest or stomach, feel the rise and fall of your breath, and gently say, "My spirit trusts God fully, and my body will learn to trust Him too." This is not positive affirmation; this is neurological retraining partnered with spiritual truth. When spoken calmly and consistently, it begins to override fear-based bodily reactions with truth-based reassurance.

Next, practice grounding techniques that reconnect your body to the present moment instead of reacting to the past. Instead of forcing yourself to "calm down," you will give your body something tangible to anchor itself to, such as pressing your feet firmly into the floor, feeling the weight of a pillow or blanket against your legs, or holding an object with texture. These physical anchors help your nervous system remember, "I am here, not back there." They help separate memories from reality.

Then, integrate scripture that speaks directly to both body and spirit, choosing verses that address rest, peace, and wholeness. When your body feels out of control, speak scriptures like: "Be at rest once more, O my soul, for the Lord has been good to you."

This verse teaches your body that rest is not earned, it is given. **"He will keep you in perfect peace."** This verse gives your nervous system permission to slow down. **"My body will rest in hope."** This verse reminds your physical being that hope is not abstract; it is an anchor.

Finally, remind yourself that body-blame is counterproductive to healing. Shame increases adrenaline; compassion decreases it. Treat your body as a loyal but confused friend, not an enemy. Say to yourself, "I do not need to punish my body for reacting. I will comfort it while it learns." Healing comes through consistency, not condemnation.

HOLY SPIRIT CONSULT

The Holy Spirit understands the complexity of your internal world more deeply than you do. He sees the places where fear took root in your body long before your spirit ever learned truth. He knows the moments where you flinched before you understood why, the nights you trembled without comfort, the days your nerves carried what your mind couldn't articulate. In this consultation, He does not shame you for the misalignment between spirit and body; instead, He gently addresses the parts of you that still react from old wounds. The Holy Spirit speaks to your nervous system with the same tenderness He uses to speak to your soul. He whispers, "Your spirit trusts Me deeply, and I am teaching your body to feel the safety your spirit already knows." He wraps your physical symptoms in reassurance, reminding your anxious chest and trembling breath that they do not have to bear the weight of survival anymore. He helps untangle the web of memories stored in your body, replacing fear with gentleness and tension with rest.

He ministers to you in the moments your chest tightens without explanation and your breath stumbles for no logical reason. He stands in the gap between your revelation and your reaction. He does not demand that your body instantly align with your spirit; He patiently nurtures the transformation until both begin to walk in unity. This consult is not just about spiritual instruction, it is about allowing the Holy Spirit to comfort your entire being, body included and reminding you that God is the God of your biology as much as the God of your belief.

GUIDED PRAYER

"Holy Spirit, I come before You with honesty, acknowledging that my spirit trusts You deeply while my body still reacts from old fears. You see the tension inside of me, the faith that stands strong and the nervous system that trembles without warning. I ask You to meet me

in this gap. Teach my body the safety my spirit knows so well. Calm the alarms that rise without reason. Comfort the places where fear still hides beneath the surface. Heal the memories stored in my body that my mind has forgotten but my nerves remember.

Let Your peace travel through my thoughts, my heartbeat, my breath, and my muscles. Help me release the pressure to be instantly healed and instead embrace the process You are guiding me through. Cover me in Your tenderness. Ground me in Your presence. Align my entire being, spirit, soul, and body, with Your peace. Amen."

REFLECTION PAGE

Questions That Restore Connection Between Spirit and Body

- What physical reactions do I experience most often when my spirit feels calm?

____

____

____

____

- What memories, environments, or past experiences might still be influencing my body's reactions?

____

____

____

____

____

____

- What truth does my spirit believe that my body needs to learn through repetition?

____

____

____

____

- How does God usually show up for me during physical anxiety symptoms?

____

____

____

- What is one way I can show compassion to my body instead of frustration?

____

____

DOCTOR'S ORDERS

Clear, Compassionate, Faith-Based Aftercare Instructions

✓ **Your body is not behind, it is healing.** Healing takes time because your nervous system learned fear through repetition, and it will unlearn fear the same way. You are not spiritually failing because your body still reacts.

✓ **Speak alignment daily.** Your body responds to tone, rhythm, and repetition. The more often you speak peace over yourself, the faster your nervous system begins to soften and trust.

✓ **Practice grounding even when you feel calm.** Healing is not only reacting in crisis; it is preparing your body to feel safe before panic begins.

✓ **Stop interpreting biology as unbelief.** A symptom is not spiritual rebellion; it is a physical pattern that God is gently rewiring.

✓ **Treat your body with compassion, not correction.** Patience reduces adrenaline. Kindness increases safety. Shame increases fear.

✓ **Trust the Holy Spirit's pacing.** He knows how to heal you without overwhelming you. Your healing is unfolding, even if slowly.

✓ **Celebrate the alignment.** Every moment your body responds with peace, even briefly, is evidence that transformation is happening at a cellular and spiritual level.

DR. PATRICIA S. TANNER

PERSONAL NOTES

92

Chapter 10:

BREATHING TECHNIQUES THAT WON'T MAKE YOU FEEL WEIRD

SYMPTOM: "I know breathing helps... but every technique I've tried makes me feel awkward, distracted, or even more anxious."

There is a unique frustration that comes with being told to "just breathe" when your nervous system is spiraling. For many people, breathing exercises don't feel natural at all, in fact, they often feel forced, mechanical, uncomfortable, or even counterproductive. You might try to inhale slowly like all the articles tell you, but your lungs rebel, your shoulders tense, and your mind become hyper-focused on "doing it right," which ironically makes your breathing worse. You might attempt the long exhales, but halfway through, your chest tightens, your throat feels thick, and instead of feeling relief, you feel trapped inside your own breathing pattern. The moment you start paying attention to your breath, you feel like you're suffocating even though nothing is wrong.

Your body wants air. Your mind wants control. Your panic wants chaos. Your spirit wants peace. And all four of these parts collide the moment you attempt slow, intentional breathing. You might feel ridiculous holding your breath for counts of four, six, or eight. You might find yourself getting annoyed when someone says, "Just breathe through it," as if breathing is not something you've done automatically since the day you were born. You might feel embarrassed that something as simple as inhaling and exhaling is suddenly 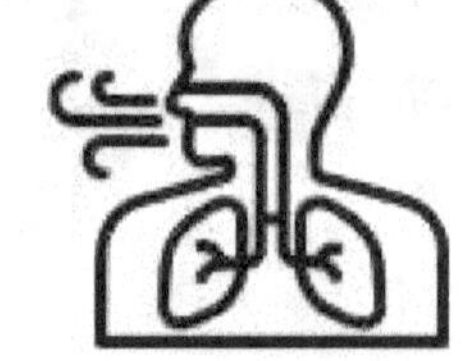 complicated. You might feel defeated because breathing exercises, which seem to help everyone else, only seem to highlight how dysregulated your body feels.

There's also the internal fear: *"What if I stop breathing correctly? What if I mess up? What if focusing on my breath makes it worse? What if I can't catch my breath at all?"* These fears create tension in the body that interrupts the natural flow of oxygen, making breathing feel like a stressful task instead of a calming tool. Some people even start panicking during breathing exercises because the act of focusing on their breath brings up memories of past panic attacks, turning the technique into a trigger rather than a relief.

This leads to shame, shame that your body should know how to do something simple, shame that breathing feels complicated, shame that you are struggling with something that seems so basic for everyone else. You begin questioning yourself, wondering why peace feels so far away and why breath feels like the hardest thing to hold onto during anxiety episodes. You may feel embarrassed, inadequate, or frustrated that you can trust God deeply and still struggle to breathe calmly in moments of distress.

Yet the real symptom is not that you "can't breathe right." The real symptom is that your nervous system is so dysregulated that intentional breathing feels foreign instead of natural. Your breath has become tied to fear, tension, and survival mode, rather than safety, calmness, and presence. Your breathing patterns were shaped in seasons of stress, trauma, or chronic overwhelm, and now your body must relearn what calm breath feels like.

TEACHING: Your Breath Is Not The Enemy, It's The Bridge Between Your Spirit And Your Nervous System

Breathing is not just a physical function. It is the most foundational, God-designed connector between your mind, your body, and your spirit. When God created Adam, He did not simply form him from the dust. He *breathed* into him. That breath was not just oxygen. It was spirit, life, presence, and connection. Your breath is holy, intentional, and deeply spiritual. It carries both biology and theology. It is both physical and supernatural.

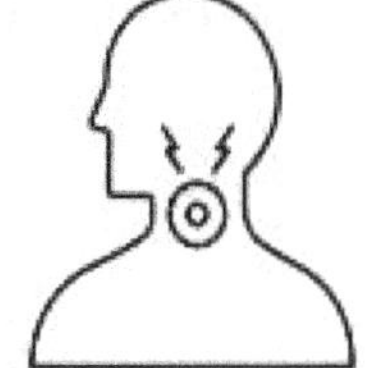

The reason panic affects your breath so quickly is because breath is the first place your nervous system checks for danger. In moments of fear, your body switches to quick, shallow breathing because it thinks you need to run or fight. It isn't trying to hurt you; it's trying to prepare you. But when you're not actually in danger, this survival mode becomes suffocating instead of protective.

Breath is the one system in your body that is both automatic and controllable, which means it's the one system that can send a signal to your brain saying, *"We're safe now."* But if breathing has been tied to panic for years, if your chest rises every time fear rises, if your throat tightens every time anxiety whispers, if your lungs constrict when trauma memories resurface, then it makes sense why breathing techniques feel unnatural or even scary.

Your body must relearn breath as a signal of peace, not danger. Many Christians dismiss breathwork because it gets associated with non-Christian practices, but the truth is that God is the One who invented breath. Jesus breathed on His disciples and said, "Receive the Holy Spirit." God breathed life into Adam. Ezekiel prophesied to *breath* in the valley of dry bones. Breath is biblical. Breath is spiritual. Breath is divine.

Breathing techniques are not weird; they are tools to retrain your nervous system so that your body begins to feel what your spirit already knows: **God is here. God is nearby. God is peace.** Your spirit believes God. Your mind trusts God. But your body needs to *experience* safety repeatedly until it rewires itself to respond to calm instead of chaos.

Healing is not about making complicated breathing patterns that feel unnatural. Healing is about learning to breathe in ways that remind your body of God's presence, not panic's memory. Your breath can become worship. Your exhale can become surrender. Your inhale can become receiving. Your breathing can become communion with God, simple, grounding, and deeply healing.

You do not need mystical techniques. You do not need complex routines. You do not need long, exhausting breath sequences. You need gentle, realistic, slow breathing patterns that your body can accept without fear, breathing exercises that do not make you feel weird, overwhelmed, self-conscious, or spiritually uncomfortable. The goal is not perfect. The goal is partnership, teaching your nervous system that God is safe, breath is safe, and you are safe.

FAITH PRESCRIPTION

1. Use the "Holy Spirit Exhale": Inhale normally. Exhale slowly while whispering, "Peace." Repeat until your shoulders lower naturally.

2. Practice "God Is Here" breathing: Inhale: "God is…" Exhale: "…here with me." This reframes breath as presence, not pressure.

3. Try the 4–2–6 calm reset: Inhale for 4 seconds. Hold for 2 Exhale for 6 Long exhale signals safety to your nervous system.

4. Hand-over-heart grounding: Place your hand on your chest Say, "We're safe now. Breathe slowly. Your body responds to reassurance.

5. Stop overthinking your breath. Your body already knows how to breathe, you're simply guiding it back to peace.

HOLY SPIRIT CONSULT

The Holy Spirit is not annoyed that your breath gets unstable. He understands the stress your lungs have carried. He understands the memories tied to shallow breath. He understands the fear that hijacks your inhale. He whispers into the chaos of your breathing, gently reminding you that He is the breath within your breath. He calms your chest with His presence, rests His peace upon your lungs, and whispers, **"Let Me breathe with you. You are not doing this alone."**

GUIDED PRAYER

"Holy Spirit, Teach me how to breathe again without fear. Rewrite the patterns in my body that panic has controlled. Let every inhale remind me that I am held and let every exhale release the fear I've carried. Fill my breath with Your presence. Calm my chest, steady my lungs, and restore peace to my body. I breathe with You, not against You. Amen."

REFLECTION PAGE

- What makes intentional breathing feel difficult for me?

____

____

____

- How has I been afraid of shaping my breathing patterns over the years?

____

____

____

- What simple breathing method feels most natural to my body?

____

____

____

- How can I use breath as a reminder of God's presence?

____

____

____

____

- What changes do I notice in my body after breathing slowly?

____

____

____

____

DOCTOR'S ORDERS

✓ Your breath is not broken, it's retraining.
✓ Slow exhale > fancy techniques.

✓ Don't force your breath; guide it gently.
✓ Use breath as spiritual practice, not a performance.

✓ God is in your inhale and your exhale.

✓ The more you practice in calm moments, the easier it becomes in anxious ones.

✓ Your breathing will become peaceful again, one slow exhale at a time.

Reflections

____

____

____

____

____

____

____

____

____

Chapter 11:

WORSHIP AS MEDICINE: SINGING WHILE SHAKING

> **SYMPTOM: "How am I supposed to worship when my hands are trembling, my voice is unsteady, and my body feels like it's falling apart?"**

There is a kind of panic that makes worship feel impossible, and yet somehow more necessary than ever. It is the moment when your body is shaking, your breath feels uneven, your voice trembles, and yet you feel this desperate longing inside your spirit to worship, to lift your hands, open your mouth, or whisper a song into a moment where your body feels like it is failing you. It feels unfair that the very times you need worship the most are often the times when your body feels the least capable of giving it. You may stand in a service, a church pew, your bedroom, or your car feeling both spiritually hungry and physically overwhelmed. Your heart wants to worship, but your body feels like it's locked in a fight for survival.

You feel the tears gathering behind your eyes, threatening to escape whether you want them to or not. Your throat tightens, not just from emotion but from the physiological tension that anxiety triggers. Your chest feels heavy, your hands tremble without warning, and even the act of lifting your arms feels strangely vulnerable. You may feel frustrated with yourself because you know worship is powerful, you know it draws you closer to God, you know it shifts

atmospheres, and you know it calms your spirit, but your body doesn't feel like participating. Your legs shake, your stomach knots, and your mind races with all the "what-ifs" that usually accompany panic: *"What if people notice? What if I collapse? What if I can't stop shaking? What if someone thinks something is wrong? What if my symptoms get worse in front of everyone?"*

In these moments, worship doesn't feel like a joyful expression, it feels like a battle. It feels like trying to sing while drowning.

It feels like reaching for God with trembling fingers. It feels like choosing faith while your body screams fear.

And the shame that sometimes surfaces only make it harder. You begin wondering, "Why is everyone else worshiping so freely while I can barely breathe? Why do my symptoms get worse the moment I walk into church? Why does my body shut down right when my spirit wants to rise?" You may feel like a spiritual fraud, like someone who "should" be able to worship with confidence but instead finds yourself gripping your seat, your shirt, or your sleeve just to feel grounded.

The truth is that worship becomes harder when your nervous system is overwhelmed, not because you lack faith, but because your body is battling fear at the exact moment your spirit is trying to press into God. Worship becomes a tug-of-war between what your spirit desires and what your body is terrified of. The shaking feels like embarrassment. The trembling feels like weakness. The inability to sing at full strength feels like failure. Yet underneath all of this is something deeply sacred, the fact that you are still reaching for God with every shaky breath, every trembling note, every whispered lyric, every tear that falls, every moment your hands rise even while your muscles tremble.

You are not weak; you are worshiping from the battlefield. This symptom is not a failure of faith but the evidence of a body still learning how to function in safety. Your trembling hands are not rebellion; they are survival instincts. Your unsteady voice is not a lack of trust; it is a nervous system doing its best. Your shaky breath is not spiritual immaturity; it is the residue of past moments where your lungs learned to fear instead of rest.

Worship while shaking is not less worship. Worship while trembling is not disqualified worship. Worship in weakness is not embarrassing worship. Worship in anxiety is worship God cherishes. Because anyone can worship God when their body feels steady. But worshiping God when everything in you is shaking? That is worship in its purest form.

TEACHING: Your Trembling Does Not Silence Your Worship, It Amplifies It.

Worship is not built on physical strength, emotional stability, or nervous system regulation. Worship is built on surrender, honesty, and connection to God. The world has conditioned us to believe that worship must look a certain way, hands raised without shaking, voice strong without cracking, body steady without trembling, breath smooth without interruption. But the Bible paints a very different picture of worship. Throughout Scripture, men and women worshiped God while afraid, overwhelmed, trembling, grieving, shaking, crying, running, hiding, hurting, bleeding, or breaking and God called it holy.

David worshiped while hunting. Hannah worshiped while weeping. Paul worshiped while imprisoned. Jehoshaphat worshiped while terrified. Jesus worshiped His Father in Gethsemane while sweating blood. Worship was never meant to come only from strength; it was designed to come from surrender.

When anxiety affects your body, your worship may feel physically weak but spiritually powerful. The shaking hands you hide in your sleeves. They might be the most honest offering you present to God. The trembling voice that barely makes it through a verse. It might be what heaven hears the loudest. The quivering knees, the shallow breath, the pounding heart, none of these disqualify your worship.

They reveal the depth of it. Your body may be responding to fear, but your spirit is responding to God.

This chapter teaches you that worship is a tool, not a performance. It is medicine, not a stage act. When your body shakes in worship, it is not betraying your spirit, it is revealing how deeply your spirit longs for safety, stability, and God's presence. Worship is one of the few practices that speaks directly to both the spirit and the nervous system. Singing slows your breath. Music regulates your emotions. Lyrics anchor your mind. Rhythm grounds your body. Presence calms your fear.

Worship is one of the most biological forms of spiritual warfare: Your lungs expand when they want to tighten. Your mouth opens when fear wants it closed. Your hands lift when your nerves want to curl inward. Your eyes look up when panic wants them darting around the room. Your body enters God's presence even when it feels afraid of being present anywhere. And here is the truth that your trembling body needs time to learn: Your worship does not depend on your physical steadiness, it depends on your willingness to show up anyway.

Worship breaks panic's control not because you feel confident, but because you surrender even while scared. Worship reconditions

your nervous system through repetition. The more you worship while shaking, the more your body learns that trembling is no danger, it is simply unfinished healing. Over time, your body begins to interpret worship as safety instead of exposure, as grounding instead of threat, as comfort instead of chaos.

God receives worship from shaking hands with the same delight as worship from steady ones. Perhaps with even more tenderness, because He knows the cost. You are not worshiping wrong. You are worshiping bravely.

FAITH PRESCRIPTION

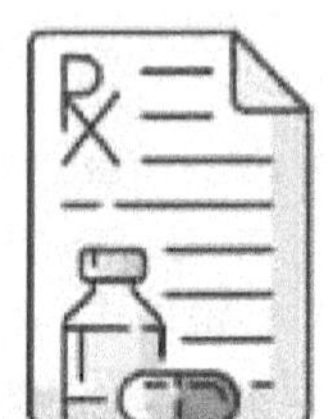 Your prescription in this chapter is not about forcing your body to be still or attempting to worship with the kind of confidence you do not currently feel. It is about learning to worship in a way that partners with your nervous system instead of competing with it. The first step is to lower the pressure. You do not need to lift your hands perfectly. You do not need to sing loudly. You do not need to match anyone else's expression. Your worship prescription begins with lowering expectations from performance to presence. You will say to yourself, "I'm not worshiping perfectly. I'm worshiping honestly."

Start with **micro-worship**, which means choosing the smallest possible act of worship you can offer without overwhelming your body. This may be as simple as whispering one line of a worship song. It may be placing your hand over your heart and saying, "God, I'm here." It might be humming, rocking gently, closing your eyes, or even just breathing slowly while music plays. Micro-worship reminds your body that worship does not demand physical strength, it invites spiritual safety.

Next, practice **grounded worship**, where you anchor your physical body so your spirit can worship without fear. Sit down instead of standing. Hold onto the back of a chair. Keep your feet firmly on the ground. Wrap yourself in a blanket if needed. Support your elbows on your knees. Stabilize your body so that your trembling doesn't feel like a threat. This teaches your nervous system that worship is a stable environment.

Then, integrate **breath-led worship**, where breath becomes part of your worship instead of something anxiety uses against you. While music plays, inhale gently on the instrumental and exhale slowly through the lyrics. This technique not only regulates your nervous system but also aligns your breathing with the rhythm of worship. It transforms your breath into participation, not pressure.

Finally, incorporate **scriptural worship**, choosing verses that speak directly to trembling, fear, surrender, and God's nearness in vulnerability. Whisper scriptures like: "The Lord is close to the brokenhearted." "My flesh and my heart may fail, but God is the strength of my heart." "In my weakness, His strength is made perfect." Scripture anchors your trembling in truth, reminding your body that worship is not dependent on steadiness, it is dependent on surrender.

Your prescription is simple: worship small, worship supported, worship with breath, worship with scripture, and worship without shame. Your body will learn through repetition that trembling does not disqualify you, it invites God to meet you where you are.

HOLY SPIRIT CONSULT

The Comfort of God in the Middle of Your Quivering Offering
The Holy Spirit approaches you during trembling worship with compassion deeper than human understanding. He does not look at your shaking hands with frustration. He does not hear your unsteady voice with disappointment. He does not see your trembling body as a lack of faith. Instead, He comes close to your weakness with tenderness, protective presence, and divine reassurance. He whispers into your trembling, "I am here, even in this."

During this consultation, the Holy Spirit reveals that He is not moved by the volume of your worship but by the vulnerability of it. He sees the cost of each note you force through shaking breath. He sees the courage it takes to whisper His name when your lungs feel tight. He sees the bravery required to lift your hands when your arms tremble under invisible weight. The Holy Spirit honors your trembling worship because He knows the battles you fought to even show up.

He sits beside you, wraps His presence around your shaking muscles, and steadies you by simply being nearby. He breathes peace into the spaces where anxiety has camped for too long. He assures you that He is not looking for polished worship. He is looking for surrendered hearts. He reminds you that He delights in the authenticity of the worshiper who brings Him trembling hands more than the one who brings Him perfect performance.

The Holy Spirit transforms your trembling into testimony. He turns your shaking into strength. He turns your unsteady breath into communion. He turns your fear into an altar. In His presence, shaking becomes worship, weakness becomes offering, and surrender becomes healing.

GUIDED PRAYER

"Holy Spirit, I come before You with a trembling body but a willing heart. My hands may shake, my voice may waver, and my breath may stumble, but I offer You everything I have in this moment. Teach me how to worship without needing to feel strong. Remind me that You receive every shaky note with joy. Wrap me in Your presence so deeply that my fear loses its power. Let my trembling become testimony. Let my weakness become worship. Let my shaking become surrender. I do not worship You because I feel steady; I worship You because You are steady. Meet me here, in the middle of my trembling, and teach my body the safety my spirit already knows. Amen."

REFLECTION PAGE

Questions to Help Your Body and Spirit Connect Through Worship

- What physical sensations do I feel when I try to worship during anxiety?

\
\
\
\
\

- What fears often rise when I attempt to sing, lift my hands, or worship publicly?

\
\
\
\

- How might micro-worship help me engage with God when full worship feels overwhelming?

\
\
\

- What scriptures comfort me the most when my body feels weak or shaky?

- What moments in the past have shown me that God meets me in my trembling, not after it?

DOCTOR'S ORDERS

Clear, Compassionate Aftercare for Worshiping Through Anxiety
✓ **Lower your expectations, worship is about presence, not performance.** Your shaky whisper is just as holy as someone else's loud shout.

✓ **Start small, micro-worship is still worship.** One lyric. One breath. One lifted hand. God notices it all.

✓ **Stabilize your body, grounded worship calms your nervous system.** Sitting, leaning, holding onto something, these are not weaknesses; they are strategies.

✓ **Use your breath as a partner, not a problem.** Slow breathing during worship reduces fear's intensity.

✓ **Stop comparing your worship posture to anyone else's.** They are not fighting your battle; you are giving God an offering they cannot see.

✓ **Repeat worship practices outside of crisis moments.** Repetition teaches your body that worship is safe.

✓ **Remember: trembling does not disqualify you.** It magnifies God's tenderness toward you.

PERSONAL REFLECTIONS

112

Chapter 12:

THE POWER OF NAMING YOUR PANIC INSTEAD OF RUNNING FROM IT

SYMPTOM: "I feel something coming... but instead of naming it, I run from it, and running makes it worse."

There is a very specific moment in anxiety that every person who struggles with panic knows too well, the moment when you feel the panic rising long before it fully arrives. It begins subtly, almost quietly, like a whisper in the back of your mind or a flutter in your chest that says, "Something's wrong." Your stomach tightens ever so slightly. Your breath becomes the tiniest bit uneven. Your thoughts shift in tone, not loud yet, just uneasy. And instead of pausing to identify what is happening, your instinct is to escape it. You rush to distract yourself. You jump to conclusions. You try to talk to yourself out of it. You fear. You run mentally, emotionally, spiritually, and sometimes physically.

This running, this immediate retreat from the feeling, turns the mild sensation into a full panic response. When you don't name the panic, your brain fills in the blanks with the worst possible scenarios: "What if this time something really is wrong?" "What if I'm about to lose control?" "What if this is the one panic attack I won't come back from?" "What if this feeling means danger?" "What if this spirals like last time?" Because you didn't name it, your brain assumes it must be something bigger, something scarier, something threatening. Ignoring or running from panic is like running from a shadow. Your body detects fear in your fleeing, not the truth in your spirit. Running communicates danger. Avoidance tells the nervous system, *"We're not safe." Silence tells the anxious part of the brain, "You're in trouble."*

Before you know it, what started as a mild wave of discomfort becomes a tidal wave of fear. Your breath starts racing even though nothing is wrong. Your vision narrows even though you're in no danger. Your chest tightens not because you're dying but because your body is preparing for a fight that does not exist. Your mind spirals not because the threat is real but because avoidance amplifies uncertainty into catastrophe.

Naming your panic feels counterintuitive because everything inside of you screams, "Don't acknowledge this! Don't look at it! Don't make it real!" But the truth is that panic grows in silence. It strengthens in avoidance. It feeds on ambiguity. It thrives in the shadow of unspoken fear. You feel ashamed to name it, afraid to acknowledge it, embarrassed to admit it, even to yourself, because you associate naming with defeat. But the real power lies in the opposite direction: panic loses its authority the moment you call it what it is. The moment you say, "This is anxiety," or "This is panic," or "I've felt this before and survived it," the fear begins to lose oxygen.

Naming panic does not admit weakness. It is reclaiming control. Naming panic is not giving it power. It is taking its power away. Naming panic is not fear-based. It is faith-based. Naming panic interrupts the spiral. Naming panic reminds your brain of reality. Naming panic tells your nervous system that you are not confused. Naming panic stops the runaway train of catastrophic thoughts before they can take over.

This chapter is about confronting the habit of running from panic, and learning the holy, healing, stabilizing art of naming it instead.

Your brain is wired for survival, which means it reacts strongly anytime something feels unfamiliar, uncomfortable, or uncertain. When a sensation rises that your brain cannot immediately categorize, it labels the unknown as dangerous. But when you name the feeling, you give your brain clarity. Naming removes mystery. Naming brings grounding. Naming restores your authority.

God created humans with the power to name things, and naming has  always been a spiritual act. In Genesis, God brought the animals to Adam and invited him to name each one. God didn't name them Himself; He gave Adam the authority to determine identity. Naming was not just a task; it was an act of dominion. It was God teaching humanity: **"You have the power to define what you are dealing with."**

Panic is no different. When you refuse to name what you are feeling, panic becomes a nameless giant. It becomes a vague, undefined threat, and the nervous system reacts to it as if it is truly something catastrophic. The unknown activates the survival response. But when you name it, "This is anxiety," "This is my nervous system misfiring," "This is panic, not danger," "This is a familiar sensation, not an emergency" your brain categorizes it properly and stops escalating the reaction.

Naming transforms fear from a monster into a manageable moment. Naming turns the floodlight on the shadows. Naming introduces truth into the tornado. Naming makes the threat shrink back into reality. Avoidance, on the other hand, teaches your body the opposite lesson. When you run, your nervous system interprets running as confirmation that there really was a threat. The next time panic rises, the reaction is even stronger because your body remembers, "Last time we ran." Avoidance strengthens the panic pathway. Naming weakens it.

Naming also interrupts spiritual shame. Many believers assume that panic is equivalent to claiming it or receiving it, but biblically, acknowledging a battle is not the same as accepting defeat. Jesus

Himself named feelings: He named sorrow. He named anguish. He named distress. He named trouble. He even named His sweat turning to blood.

Naming is not unspiritual; it is holy honesty. When you name your panic, you are not glorifying fear; you are exposing lies. You are not empowering anxiety; you are disarming it. You are not claiming panic; you are clarifying your experience so you can reclaim your authority over it.

Spiritually, naming panic invites God into the exact place where the fear lives. You cannot surrender what you will not name. You cannot heal what you refuse to identify. You cannot cast down what remains vague and unspoken. Naming your panic is saying, "Lord, this is what I'm feeling. I bring it into the light. I hand it to You. I ask You to meet me here." God does not require perfection before presence. He requires honesty before healing. Nothing becomes unspiritual simply because you name it. In fact, nothing becomes healable until you name it. Your spirit already knows what your body is experiencing. Your mind already senses when something is rising. But naming pulls all three, spirit, soul, and body, into alignment so that panic is no longer navigating your inner world in the dark.

Naming panic is not running toward fear, it is standing still long enough to tell fear that you are no longer afraid of acknowledging its presence. And that is where the power begins.

FAITH PRESCRIPTION

Your prescription here is to develop a three-step naming habit that interrupts panic before it escalates:

1. Identify it out loud: In a soft, steady voice say, **"This is panic.**

This is not danger. My body is reacting, not warning me." Out-loud naming interrupts the limbic system and activates logical reasoning.

2. Describe what's happening inside your body: Not in fear, in clarity. Example: "My chest feels tight, but this has happened before." "My thoughts are racing, but they will slow down." "My breath is shallow, but I can control my exhale." Naming sensations re-engages the thinking brain.

3. Reassure yourself with truth: "This is temporary." "This will pass." "I have survived this before." "God is with me right now." Truth breaks the fear loop. Use this every time panic whispers, not after it shouts.

HOLY SPIRIT CONSULT

The Holy Spirit comes close the moment you name your panic. He does not wait until you feel brave. He meets you at the first stutter of fear. When you say, "This is panic," He gently responds, "And I am here." His presence fills the place where your fear used to escalate. He honors your courage to speak honestly. He strengthens your heart when you feel weak. He steadies your breath when it feels uneven. He wraps your trembling body in peace and reminds you that naming your panic does not amplify fear, it invites Him closer. He whispers: **"You are safe. You are not alone. Your fear is not bigger than My presence. I am proud of you for naming what scared you. Let Me carry the weight of this moment."** Naming panic becomes the doorway for His nearness.

GUIDED PRAYER

"Holy Spirit, Teach me not to run from my panic but to name it with confidence. Help me speak truth over my body when fear begins to rise. Give me the courage to say what I am feeling without shame.

Let Your presence fills the room the moment I name my anxiety. Turn my honesty into strength. Turn my naming into healing. I refuse to hide from what scares me. I place it in Your hands, and I let Your peace rewrite my reaction. Amen."

REFLECTION PAGE

Bring your fear into the light, one question at a time

- What physical sensations do I feel before panic fully rises?

____

____

- What thoughts begin to whisper when anxiety starts?

____

____

- Why do I fear naming what I feel?

____

____

- How has avoidance made my panic worse over time?

____

____

- What truth can I say the next time fear starts to build?

DOCTOR'S ORDERS

Naming is healing, not weakness

✓ Name it early, before the spiral grows.
✓ Speak out loud, silence feeds fear.
✓ Describe sensations without judgment.
✓ Reassure your body with truth, not shame.
✓ Invite God into the moment immediately.
✓ Remember: naming is dominion, avoidance is fear.
✓ You take back power every time you say, "This is panic, not danger."

Reflections

Chapter 13:

REWRITING YOUR BODY'S STORY: RESTORATION FROM THE INSIDE OUT

SYMPTOM: "My spirit has moved on, but my body is still stuck in old chapters it never finished reading."

There is a kind of pain that doesn't live in your thoughts anymore but remains lodged inside your body. You no longer think the way you used to think. You no longer believe the lies you used to believe. You are spiritually stronger, emotionally wiser, mentally healthier, and far more grounded than you once were. You know God more intimately. You trust Him more deeply. You recognize His voice more clearly. You've grown. You've healed. You've matured. But your body has not caught up to the new story.

Your body is still tense in places where you now feel safe. Your  chest still tightens in conversations that no longer threaten you. Your breath still changes when nothing is wrong. Your shoulders still rise involuntarily when you hear certain tones of voice. Your stomach still knots when someone asks, "Can we talk?" Your nerves still fire when people approach too quickly. Your heart still races when your phone rings unexpectedly.

None of these reactions match your current reality, they match your past one. Your spirit is living in a new chapter, but your body is still rereading an old one. And that disconnect is painful and deeply discouraging. You begin to wonder, "Why do I still react this way if I've healed?" "Why does my body still behave like something bad is about to happen?" "Why does it feel like my body remembers things I've tried so hard to forget?" "Why is my body stuck in a chapter God already rewrote?"

The truth is simple: Your body carries a story your spirit has already outgrown. Your nerves learned survival before they learned trust. Your breath learned fear before it learned peace. Your muscles learned vigilance before they learned safety. Your heartbeat learned panic before it learned stillness. Your biology was shaped by experiences that trained your body to anticipate danger, even when danger no longer exists. This doesn't make you weak. This doesn't make you broken. This doesn't mean your healing "didn't work." This doesn't mean your faith is counterfeit. It means your body is still living inside a narrative that your spirit has already rewritten with God.

The symptom here is not recurring fear. It is recurring memory, memory stored in muscles, breath, hormones, and reflexes that haven't yet been updated to match the new reality God has brought you into.

Your body is not resisting healing; it is requesting restoration. Not just spiritual restoration. Not just emotional restoration. Not just mental restoration. But **somatic** restoration. Deep restoration. Cellular restoration. From the inside out. Your body is waiting for permission to let go of a story it has carried for years. And this chapter is about teaching it how.

TEACHING: Your Body Remembers What Your Spirit Has Forgotten, And God Restores Both.

Your spirit grows through revelation. Your soul grows through understanding. Your mind grows through renewal. But your body grows through repetition, rewiring, and regulated experiences of safety. This means healing is not just spiritual, it is holistic. You cannot simply pray away what your biology learned through years of distress. You cannot shout scriptures at a nervous system shaped by  trauma and expect it to instantly forget everything it endured.

You cannot command your breath to calm when it has spent years associating shallow breathing with survival. Your body does not speak theology. It speaks memory. And that memory lives in your fascia, your nervous system, your gut, your reflexes, your breathing patterns, your postures, your tension points, your heartbeat rhythms, and your startle responses.

 This is why someone raising their voice, even harmlessly, can cause your chest to tighten. This is why a sudden sound can make your muscles jump. This is why someone walking behind you makes your shoulders rise. This is why conflict makes your stomach churn. This is why intimacy triggers adrenaline. This is why a harmless conversation can activate panic. This is why silence feels threatening.

Your spirit says, "We are safe." Your body says, "Prove it." But healing is not about forcing your body to "get over it." Healing is about helping your body update its story. God does not just heal wounds, He rewrites narratives. He goes to places where fear taught your body to expect the worst. He goes to the moments where abandonment taught your nervous system to brace for loss. He goes to the seasons where betrayal trained your muscles to anticipate pain. He goes to the nights where panic hardwired itself into your breath. And He begins the long, patient, holy work of restoring your body from the inside out.

He does this through: **Presence**; which softens tension **Truth**; which calms the fear response **Repetition**; which retrains patterns **Worship**; which regulates the nervous system **Stillness**; which teaches the body that peace is possible **Naming**; which brings clarity to the unknown **Surrender**; which resets the inner alarms **Rest**; which teaches safety instead of threat.

Restoration is not instant. Restoration is not linear. Restoration is not rushed. Restoration is not loud. Restoration is slow, sacred, embodied work. Restoration is breathing new life into old reflexes.

Restoration is teaching your body to unlearn tension. Restoration helps your muscles stop expecting pain. Restoration is letting God rewrite your body's reactions, patterns, and reflexes so that your physical responses finally align with your spiritual reality. Your spirit has already turned the page. Now your body is learning how to follow.

FAITH PRESCRIPTION

Training Your Body to Live in the Chapter Your Spirit Already Knows

1. Speak a new narrative over your body. Place your hand over your chest or stomach and say: "Body, we are safe now. That chapter is over. God is rewriting our story." This signals alignment, not denial.

2. Practice "safety repetitions." Every day, intentionally expose your body to calm moments, even 30 seconds at a time, to rebuild a foundation of safety.

3. Rewrite physical memory with presence. When the old tension rises, instead of running, say: "This feeling is from the past. God is with me in the present."

4. Use scripture that speaks to physical restoration.
- "He restores my soul."
- "Peace be still."
- "In Him we live and move and have our being."

5. Allow yourself to rest without guilt. Rest is not laziness; it is rehabilitation for a nervous system that carried too much for too long.

HOLY SPIRIT CONSULT

The Holy Spirit does not only comfort your spirit. He comforts your biology. He sees every flinch, every tremor, every involuntary reaction that you can't explain. He knows the chapters your body still carries, the ones you stopped talking about years ago. And He speaks to your body with the same authority He speaks to your soul. He whispers into your tension: **"You don't have to brace anymore."** He speaks over your breath: **"You are safe to inhale deeply now."** He says to your muscles: **"Release what was never yours to hold."** He tells your heartbeat: **"You can slow down now. I am here."** He is the God who restores you from the inside out, not just rewriting your life but rewriting your body's memory of it.

GUIDED PRAYER

"Holy Spirit, Rewriting the story my body still believes. Heal the tension, the reflexes, the alarms, and the memories stored in my nerves. Restore me from the inside out. Teaching my body the truth my spirit already knows that I am safe, seen, loved, protected, and held. Release the old patterns, Lord. Rewire my reactions. Review my responses. Let peace become my default. Let rest become my rhythm. Let safety become my story. Amen."

REFLECTION PAGE

Questions about Embodied Healing
- What physical patterns do I notice repeating even when I'm spiritually strong?

- What chapters from my past might my body still be holding onto?

- Which sensations feel tied to memory rather than current reality?

- How has God already begun rewriting my story?

- What does physical safety feel like to me?

DOCTOR'S ORDERS

Restoration Requires Repetition

✓ Don't shame your body for remembering, teach it gently.

✓ Speak truth to your physical sensations, not fear.

✓ Rest is medicine for your nervous system.

✓ You will not always react this way, your body is healing.

✓ God is restoring you at every level, spirit, soul, and body.

✓ This chapter ends. Your new one will feel like peace.

Reflections

____

____

____

____

____

____

____

____

____

____

____

____

Chapter 14:

COMMUNITY CARE: WHEN YOU NEED SOMEONE TO SIT WITH YOUR STORM

SYMPTOM: "I don't want to be alone... but I don't know how to let anyone in while my anxiety is spiraling."

There is a specific ache that comes with anxiety, the ache of wanting help but not knowing how to ask for it. You may find yourself longing for someone to sit with you, someone to breathe beside you, someone to remind you that you're not losing your mind, someone who can be a calming presence in a moment where everything inside of you feels frantic. And yet, in the same breath, you fear letting anyone see you in that condition. It feels vulnerable, exposed, risky, and even humiliating. You want comfort, but you fear being a burden. You want presence, but you feel like a problem. You want to reach out, but you don't want to "make it a big deal."

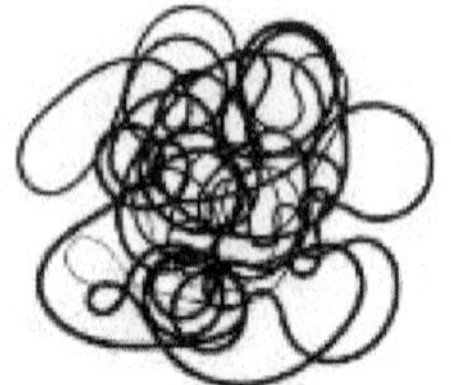

When panic rises, the instinct is to isolate, not because you want to be alone, but because anxiety convinces you that no one will understand. You don't want people to see your shaking hands, hearing your trembling voice, or watching you struggle to breathe. You fear being misunderstood. You fear being judged. You fear making others uncomfortable. You fear someone thinking you're being dramatic or overly emotional. You fear calling someone for help and hearing the disappointment in their tone or the impatience in their sight.

There's also the internal conflict: "If I reach out, am I weak?" "If I need help, does that mean I don't have enough faith?" "If I can't calm myself down, does that make me a burden?" "If someone sees me like this, will they think less of me?" So, you sit alone in your storm, shaking, crying, spiraling, trying to hold yourself together, while your heart silently pleads, "I wish someone was here." And even in community spaces, you may feel alone in the middle of a crowd. People see your smile but not your trembling hands tucked inside your pocket. They hear your laugh but not the panic vibrating beneath your ribs. You may even sit among friends who love you but still feel like you are drowning in the shallow end of your own fear.

You may long deeply for someone to sit with you during your storm, to place a steadying hand on your back, to pray with you, to whisper truth over your shaking body, to be a human reminder of God's nearness. And yet, letting someone into that space feels terrifying. It feels like giving them backstage access to your most raw, unfiltered self.

The symptom here is the tension between wanting connection and fearing vulnerability, between craving support and believing you don't deserve it, between needing community and convincing yourself you should heal alone.

But storms were never meant to survive in isolation. Even Jesus asked His closest friends to sit with Him in the garden. You're not weak in needing someone. You're human.

TEACHING: Your Healing Accelerates When Your Storm Is Witnessed, Not Hidden.

God created healing to be communal. From Genesis to Revelation, healing rarely happens in isolation. Breakthroughs happen in community. Strength is shared in community. Comfort is exchanged in community. Even Jesus, perfect, holy, divine, invited people into His most vulnerable moments. He asked  His disciples, *"Stay here with Me."* Not because He couldn't handle the storm alone, but to show us that even the Son of God embraced communal presence in moments of distress.

DR. PATRICIA S. TANNER

 When you are isolated during panic, the storm inside your mind grows louder. Anxiety thrives in silence. Fear multiplies in secrecy. Thoughts become distorted when they have no one to challenge them. Panic becomes more convincing when it is the only voice you hear. Community isn't a luxury; it is a stabilizer. It grounds you in reality. It anchors you in truth. It reminds you that fear is not your only companion.

You were designed for regulated nervous systems, safe relationships, and comforting presence. When you sit with someone who is calm, your body begins to mirror their stability. This is not psychology, this is creation. God designed the human body so that "presence regulates presence." When someone sits with you, your heart rate slows. When someone speaks gently to you, your breath deepens. When someone prays over you, your nervous system begins to soften. Community care is not optional; it is necessary.

Many believers misunderstand this. They think faith means handling storms alone. They think asking for help is weakness. They think needing someone's presence means they're spiritually immature. But the Bible tells a different story. Paul leaned on the church. David surrounded himself with warriors. Naomi leaned on Ruth. Moses needed Aaron and Hur to hold up his arms. Elijah needed the angel to touch him. Jesus needed His friends in Gethsemane.

Healing is not a solo sport. Faith is not isolation. Deliverance is not distance. Breakthrough is not independent. Your storm becomes survivable when someone else sits in it with you. Community care is the antidote to panic's isolation. It teaches your body: "I am not alone. I am not in danger. There is a witness to my storm. There is someone here with me." And something powerful happens when someone sits with you, the storm loses its intensity.

Panic stops feeling infinite. Fear stops feeling immortal. You stop believing lies whispered in the dark. Community brings the storm into the light, and darkness loses its voice in the presence of connection. Healing from the inside out requires others not to fix you, but to sit with you.

FAITH PRESCRIPTION

Let someone hold space for your storm, without shame.
1. Identify one or two safe people. Not everyone can handle your storm, but someone can. Choose individuals who make you feel seen, not judged.

2. Create a "panic plan." Tell your safe person what helps you during anxiety:
- "Just sit with me."
- "Pray softly."
- "Help me breathe."
- "Don't preach at me."
- "Remind me I'm safe."

3. Practice reaching out BEFORE the storm peaks. Text or call the moment your symptoms begin, not after you're overwhelmed.

4. Allow presence to do what words cannot. You don't need someone to *fix* you. You need them to *stay with you.*

5. Build community care into your healing rhythm. Schedule regular check-ins. Share victories and setbacks. Let people help carry the weight.

HOLY SPIRIT CONSULT

The Holy Spirit never shames you for needing human presence. In fact, He often orchestrates it. He nudges hearts, aligns timing, and brings the right people into your world at the right moments. He whispers, *"Let them sit with you. Let them carry some of this. You were not built to break alone."* He reminds you that community is not a sign of weakness but a gift of grace. He surrounds you with people who reflect His nature, comforters, encouragers, burden-bearers, truth-speakers. He sits with you through them. He comforts you through them. He speaks peace through them. Their presence becomes His presence extended. The Holy Spirit is not calling you to isolation. He is drawing you toward safety in numbers.

GUIDED PRAYER

"Holy Spirit, I admit that I struggle to let people into my storms. I fear being a burden, I fear being misunderstood, I fear being seen in my shaking and vulnerability. But I also know I was not meant to heal alone. Teach me how to reach out. Show me the people You have assigned to sit with me. Give me the courage to invite support when my storm begins. Let community become part of my healing And let connection become a shelter for my anxious body. Amen."

REFLECTION PAGE

Bringing Your Storm Into Relationship

- *Who in my life feels emotionally safe and spiritually grounded?*

____

____

____

- *What fears keep me from asking for support during panic moments?*

____

____

____

- How has isolation increased my anxiety in the past?

____

____

____

- *What type of support do I need during a storm?*

____

____

____

- *How might God be inviting me into deeper community care?*

____

____

____

DOCTOR'S ORDERS

Healing Happens Faster When You Heal Together
✓ Stop isolating, storms shrink when witnessed.
✓ Pick safe people and tell them how to help.

✓ Reach out early, not just when panic peaks.

✓ Presence heals what words can't.

✓ Community doesn't replace God, it reflects Him.

✓ You're not a burden; you're a human being.

✓ Let people sit with you, that's how storms lose their power.

Reflections

____

____

____

____

____

____

____

____

____

____

Epilogue:
YOU'RE NOT BROKEN, YOU'RE BEING REBUILT

DR. PATRICIA S. TANNER

The Gospel According to Sweaty Palms, Racing Hearts, and a God Who Never Leaves the Room

There is a moment in the healing journey where you finally look back and realize something profound: the panic that once ruled your body no longer gets to narrate your life. It may still be speaking. It may still whisper. It may still try to rise at inconvenient times. But

it no longer gets the microphone. It no longer gets the final say. It no longer drags you into darkness without resistance. You have learned how to show up in your own body with authority. You have learned how to breathe through storms with wisdom. You have learned how to anchor yourself in truth instead of terror. And maybe most powerful of all, you have learned that God never once abandoned you in the shaking.

If this book has done anything, I hope it taught you this: your panic attacks do not disqualify you from peace, purpose, or the presence of God. They do not disqualify you from strength. They do not disqualify you from healing. They do not disqualify you from community. And they do not disqualify you from being used by God. You are not spiritually defective because your body spirals. You are not "less saved" because your breath catches. You are not weak because your chest tightens. You are not unfaithful because your nervous system has triggers. You are not lacking in faith because your biology remembers pain differently than your spirit does.

You are a fully human being walking with a fully present God. And He is not intimidated by your symptoms. He is not rolling His eyes at your panic. He is not disappointed when you're trembling. He is not distant when your thoughts race. He is not pacing heaven wondering why you can't "get it together." He is close. He is near. He is invested. He is inside your storm with you.

You have learned what most believers never dare admit out loud: your body can panic while your faith stands firm. The two can coexist, and you can still move forward. You can still heal. You can still function. You can still love God. You can still trust Him, even while your biology occasionally misfires.

This journey has shown you that anxiety is not a spiritual indictment, it is a physiological pattern with a spiritual companion. You've learned how to name it, how to calm it, how to breathe through it, how to pray through it, how to worship through it, and how to let others sit with you in the storm. You've learned that you can be trembling and triumphant at the same time. You can be healing and holy at the same time. You can be anxious and annoyed at the same time.

What God is doing in you is not small. It is not surface level. It is not temporary. It is not accidental. This is full restoration. This is inside-out healing. This is the rebuilding of reflexes, memories, narratives, and nervous systems. This is the redemption of your breath, your heartbeat, your muscles, and your inner alarms. This is God teaching your biology what your spirit already knows, you are safe. you are seen. you are carried. you are His.

And now, something new is unfolding you are learning to trust not just God with your soul, but God with your body. You are learning to let Him rewrite your physical responses, your reflexive reactions, your stress patterns, your emotional rhythms. You are learning to let Him be Lord over fear, not just in theory, but in the chemistry of your cells. You are learning to let Him into the places you once hid, the places you once feared, the places you thought healing couldn't reach.

Nothing in your story is wasted. Not shaking. Not sleepless nights. Not the racing thoughts. Not the panic attacks in church bathrooms. Not the shallow breathing in parking lots. Not the breakdowns you prayed no one would notice. Not the trembling you wrapped in silence. God is using every moment as material, not to shame you, but to reconstruct you.

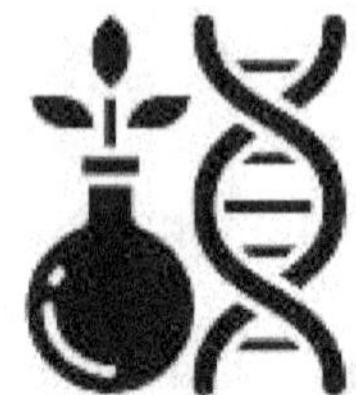 Healing doesn't mean the absence of panic; it means the presence of power. Healing doesn't mean you never tremble again; it means you don't tremble alone. Healing doesn't mean you never feel anxious; it means anxiety no longer gets to be your shepherd. You have a Shepherd, a good one, who walks with you through valleys, panic attacks, and tight-breathed nights. You have a Comforter who doesn't wait outside the storm but enters it with you. You have a Father who isn't disgusted by your fear but draws near to it. You have a Savior who understands distress and meets you inside of it.

So here is your final reminder: You are not broken, you are rebuilding. You are not failing, you are healing. You are not behind, you are becoming. You are not alone, you are held. And the next time your palms get sweaty, your chest gets tight, your breath gets shallow, or your nerves start whispering lies, you will not crumble. You will not run. You will not hide. You will not panic about the panic.

You will say: "My body is remembering something God already delivered me from, but I'm safe. He is here. And this storm is not my story." Because you, yes, *you*, are living proof that trembling people can walk with a steady God. You are the testimony. You are the chapter heaven is writing. You are the evidence that anxiety does not get to win. And this is the beginning of a new ending, the kind where fear loses, faith rises, and you walk out of the storm without apology, without shame, and without the lie that panic gets the final say.

You are healing. You are whole. You are His.

FAITH CLINIC: OFFICIAL DISCHARGE INSTRUCTIONS

"You're Released, But You're Not Walking Out Empty-Handed."
Panic Attacks Edition: When Your Spirit Says "Trust God," but
Your Body Hits the Emergency Button

PATIENT NAME: ________________________________

DATE OF RELEASE: ________________________________

I. YOUR FINAL DIAGNOSIS

Not broken, just overloaded.
- Nervous system trained by old chapters
- Body reacting to memories your spirit has outgrown
- Anxiety misinterpreted as danger
- Panic loops triggered by unprocessed stress
- Faith intact, identity intact, spirit grounded

This discharge confirms what the enemy never wanted you to know:
**You were never the problem, your patterns were. And patterns
can be retrained.**

II. SUMMARY OF TREATMENT PROVIDED

Over the course of this spiritual hospitalization, you have:
✓ Learned to name your panic instead of running from it
✓ Rewritten your body's story with truth instead of fear
✓ Practiced breathing without shame
✓ Worshiped while shaking
✓ Embraced micro-trust and microscopic courage
✓ Allowed God into your biology, not just your theology
✓ Learned that community care is not weakness

✓ Discovered that your spirit can stay steady even when your body spirals. Your progress is significant and medically miraculous.

III. WHAT TO EXPECT POST-DISCHARGE

Healing is not overnight, it is ongoing.

❖ Occasional shaking? Normal.

❖ Random tightness in your chest? Expected.

❖ Racing thoughts out of nowhere? Not a setback.

❖ Wobbly knees during worship? Not spiritual failure.

❖ Needing help from others? Biblical.

You are not relapsing; your nervous system is recalibrating. Healing is happening even when it feels slow.

IV. HOME CARE INSTRUCTIONS

1. Breathing Practice, Non-Negotiable

• **4-count inhale, 6-count exhale** Repeat for 2–3 minutes, twice daily. Exhales calm your nervous system; this is not "optional," it's neurological medicine.

2. Micro-Worship Worship does not require strength, only honesty. **Humming, whispering lyrics, or placing your hand over your heart** counts. Repeat daily.

3. Panic Naming Protocol

When symptoms rise:

1. **Say out loud:** "This is panic, not danger."
1. **Describe it:** "My chest is tight, but I'm safe."
2. **Reassure:** "This is temporary. God is here."

This interrupts the fear loop before it escalates.

4. Body-Story Rewriting

Put your hand over your chest and speak: **"Body, you can stand down. This chapter is over. God is restoring us."** Use morning and night.

5. Community Contact
Identify two safe people:
Name 1: ___________________________
Name 2: ___________________________
Reach out early, not in crisis. Storms shrink when witnessed.

6. Scripture Stabilizers
Use these as "spiritual sedatives":
- Psalm 34:18 - He is near
- Psalm 46:10 - Be still
- Isaiah 26:3 - Perfect peace
- 2 Timothy 1:7 - Power over fear
- John 14:27 - Peace, He *gives* you

Read one before bed every night.

7. Rest (Doctor's Orders)
You are forbidden from:
• Overworking
• Stuffing your emotions
• Spiritualizing exhaustion
• Apologizing for needing rest

Your nervous system heals while you sleep, not while you grind.

V. EMERGENCY INSTRUCTIONS

In case a panic storm tries to revisit you…

1. Do NOT:

✗ Spiral alone

✗ Breathe fast

✗ Try to overpower panic

✗ Condemn yourself

✗ Assume something is physically wrong without evidence

2. DO:

✓ Sit down

✓ Put your hand over your chest

✓ Slow your exhale

✓ Speak truth out loud

✓ Text your safe person

✓ Play one worship song

✓ Invite the Holy Spirit into the moment

3. If symptoms persist

Repeat this script: **"My body is remembering something my spirit has already healed from. I am safe. I am held. God is with me."**

VI. FOLLOW-UP APPOINTMENTS

Healing has check-ins, don't skip them.
- **Weekly Self Check:** What improved? What triggered you?
- **Community Check-In:** One conversation with your safe person weekly.
- **Holy Spirit Check-In:** Daily moment of stillness. No pressure.
- **Worship Check-In:** Once a week, even if your hands shake.

VII. MEDICAL CLEARANCE FOR YOUR NEXT SEASON

You are hereby cleared to:

✓ Live with confidence

✓ Worship without fear

✓ Trust God even when your body shakes

✓ Build community that cares for your storm

✓ Name your sensations without shame
✓ Walk in peace you never thought was possible
✓ Let God finish the inside-out restoration
✓ Step boldly into your calling, panic does not own you
You are released, **but your healing continues.**

PATIENT SIGNATURE: ___________________________

ATTENDING PHYSICIAN (THE GREAT I AM): ✛ JESUS, MDIV, ALPHA & OMEGA

🗓 30-DAY HEALING PLAN

"One month of retraining your body, rebuilding your peace, and restoring your rhythm."
Daily instructions • Weekly focus • Nervous system rehab • Spiritual regulation

WEEK 1: TEACH YOUR BODY YOU'RE SAFE

Theme: Safety Before Strength

Day 1: Practice the **4-6 breathing pattern** for 3 minutes. Speak out loud: *"My body is safe in this moment."*

Day 2: Identify your panic early-warning sensations (tightness, heat, tingling). Write them down. Name them. Don't run.

Day 3: Choose your **panic partner**, your safe person who will sit with you. Tell them what helps you.

Day 4: Practice micro-worship: hum, whisper, or listen to one song while seating.

Day 5: Spend 5 minutes in intentional stillness. Your only job: breathe slowly and notice tension leaving.

Day 6: Choose one scripture as your personal sedative. Repeat it out loud until your body softens.

Day 7: Take a "rest inventory" where are you exhausted? Fix one thing today.

WEEK 2: RENEW YOUR BODY'S STORY

Theme: Updating Old Reflexes

Day 8: Place your hand over your chest. Say: *"Body, we are not in danger. That chapter is over."*

Day 9: Track one panic pattern from start → peak → decline. Notice: *It always ends.*

Day 10: Do one grounding activity: Feet on floor • Warm shower • Weighted blanket • Rocking motion.

Day 11: Practice the **Naming Protocol**: "This is panic. This is not danger. I am safe."

Day 12: Try the **30-second safety repetition**: Relax shoulders → slow exhale → repeat "This moment is not a threat."

Day 13: Reflect on one moment God carried you through. Tell your body: *"See? We survived."*

Day 14: Worship while sitting. Let your voice be shaky, heaven calls it honest.

<u>WEEK 3: REBUILD YOUR TRUST SYSTEM</u>
Theme: Trust That Outlives the Trembling

Day 15: Write: "Where does my body still react like my past is present?"

Day 16: Practice "leaning presence" with someone safe, sit together for 5 minutes.

Day 17: Journal truth-over-fear statements:

- "My body is learning."
- "My fear is not prophetic."
- "My healing is not behind."

Day 18: Practice one worship breath cycle: Inhale during instrumental • Exhale during lyrics.

Day 19: Call or text your safe person, tell them one win this week.

Day 20: Do a gentle 10-minute walk while repeating a scripture on peace.

Day 21: Design your "storm plan":

- Who to call
- What to say
- What song to play
- What truth to speak
- What truth to speak

<u>WEEK 4: LIVE LIKE YOU'RE HEALING (BECAUSE YOU ARE)</u>

Theme: Peace as a Lifestyle

Day 22: Practice worship with movement, sway, tap, rock gently.

Day 23: Identify one fear-based behavior you're letting go of.

Day 24: Revisit a past trigger with someone safe (in conversation only). Notice: Your body reacts differently now.

Day 25: Commit to a "no shame day" no criticizing your symptoms.

Day 26: Do a full-body release: Relax forehead → jaw → shoulders → stomach → hands → legs.

Day 27: Speak this blessing over yourself: **"I am not fragile. I am becoming strong in new ways."**

Day 28: Worship for 3 minutes. Don't aim for pretty, aim for present.

Day 29: Write your testimony in progress (not finished, in progress).

Day 30: Celebrate. You didn't quit. You didn't fold. You didn't lose. Your body is learning peace. Your spirit stayed grounded. You made it through 30 days of rebuilding.

Reflections

____

____

____

____

____

EMERGENCY WALLET CARD

"Pull this out when your body forgets the truth."

FRONT "BREATHE. YOU'RE SAFE."

• This is panic, not danger.

• I have survived this before.

• It will pass, it always does.

• Slow exhale is my weapon.

• God is here. I am not alone.

BACK, 30-SECOND STABILIZATION

1. Exhale for 6 seconds

2. Name it: "This is panic."

3. Reassure: "My body is remembering, not warning."

4. Ground: Feel feet on floor

5. Truth: "I am safe. God is with me right now."

Emergency Contact (My Safe Person):
Name: _______________________
Phone: _______________________

FINAL READER BLESSING

"Before you close this book, let heaven speak over you."

May the God who calms storms calm the storms inside your chest. May the One who breathes life into dust breathe peace into every shallow inhale you fight through. May the Prince of Peace stand guard around your nervous system until your body finally believes the safety your spirit has known all along.

May trembling never shame you again. May panic never define you again. May fear never get the final say again. May your breath return to you soft. May your chest open without battle. May your sleep be deep and unafraid. May your mornings begin with confidence instead of dread. May God rewrite your reflexes, reset your rhythm, and restore your strength from the inside out.

And when anxiety tries to resurrect old chapters, may you remember this truth with holy stubbornness: ***"My body might shake, but my God does not."*** Walk out of this clinic braver than you came in, steadier than you expected, and more held than you realized. You are healing. You are growing. You are carried. You are safe. You are His. And this story ends in peace.

Final Reflections

____

____

____

____

____

____

____

____

ABOUT THE AUTHOR

Dr. Patricia Tanner was born and raised in Sanford FL. She comes from a family of three siblings. Patricia Tanner is the founder of Multhai International Realty, Multhai Asset Management Services, and Multhai Investment Group which is located in Sanford, Florida. She is a graduate of the University of Central Florida, where she received a Bachelor of Science in Business Administration and a minor in Human Resources Management.

Dr. Tanner began her career shortly thereafter as a Regional Property Manager in the apartment community. Throughout her career in property management, she has built interpersonal relationships with corporate clients. She has a successful track record of increasing company revenues over $5 million annually, through hard work, commitment, creativeness, and strategic planning.

Her experience and leadership role eventually led her to achieve a Florida Real Estate Broker license. She spent fifteen years in the Real Estate field while completing a Master of Arts in Human Resources Management from Webster University, and a Master of Public Administration from Troy University. It was in this capacity that she decided to open her own brokerage company, Multhai International Realty.

In addition, Dr. Tanner finds time in her busy schedule to participate in her own Non-For-Profit Organization, Stones 2 Homes. She remains President of her organization in which she helps people build, keep, or purchase homes in affordable communities. She is the founder of PNT Property Partners in which she buys vacant land, develops it, and constructs brand new construction homes in Sanford Florida. Her overall goal is to educate and provide resources to help people overcome financial hardships and credit disadvantage to live the American Dream through homeownership in spite of economic hardship. Through her visions she will continue to grow as an entrepreneur and is willing to share her knowledge, experience, and expertise with anyone who is willing to learn.

MORE BOOKS BY THE AUTHOR

Welcome to the Faith Clinic—where your soul doesn't need to be perfect to be healed.

You've smiled through burnout. Quoted scripture while quietly unraveling. Prayed, fasted, and still felt like your faith flatlined. If that's you, Faith Clinic: Volume I is your spiritual prescription.

Dr. Patricia S. Tanner—known as The Faith Doctor—invites you into a raw, grace-filled recovery journey for the soul. With 7 powerful doses of faith-infused wisdom, this book delivers healing where performance failed and offers truth where church hurt left a scar. Designed especially for spiritually exhausted youth and young adults, each "dose" reads like an IV drip of hope for believers secretly running on empty.

You don't need to be okay to show up. You just need to be willing. The clinic is open.

NOW AVAILABLE:
www.amazon.com

Healing was just the beginning. Now it's time to grow.

If Faith Clinic Volume I met you in crisis, Volume II meets you in recovery. Because faith isn't a one-time fix—it's a lifestyle that needs maintenance, accountability, and consistency. Welcome to your follow-up care plan.

In Faith Clinic: Volume II, Dr. Patricia S. Tanner—aka The Faith Doctor—guides you through the next level of your spiritual healing journey. From navigating church trauma and burnout to facing silence from God and rediscovering purpose, this book goes deeper than devotionals. It's not about hype—it's about habits that sustain real, lasting transformation.

With raw wisdom, relatable stories, and no-shame truths, each chapter is a spiritual check-in for believers who want to thrive—not just survive. Whether you're wrestling with doubt, craving stability, or simply ready to grow up in God, this clinic is for you.

You've detoxed. Now it's time to build. Let's get you discharge-ready.

NOW AVAILABLE:

www.amazon.com

Welcome to the Faith Clinic: Anxiety Edition — where God doesn't coddle your coping mechanisms but confronts them with surgical precision.

This book is for the ones who love Jesus but still can't sleep. For the worship leaders crying in church bathrooms. For the believers who pray in spirals, fight shame on Sundays, and secretly think, "Maybe I'm the only one who can't seem to breathe through this." You're not crazy. You're just in a fight — and this book is your spiritual triage.

Inside you'll find:
- Panic attacks in pews and the prayers that still work.
- Scriptures that talk you off the ledge.
- What to do when you feel numb and God feels quiet.
- How to walk out of shame loops, judgment spirals, and performance religion.

This isn't just encouragement. It's equipment.
Because healing isn't a moment — it's a walk.

NOW AVAILABLE:

www.amazon.com

Welcome to the Faith Clinic: Stress Edition — where we don't hand you cute verses and clichés. We hand you spiritual prescriptions for real pressure, real panic, and real prayers from tired believers holding it together by a thread.

This book is for the overwhelmed—those trusting God while juggling bills, burnout, hustle culture, and holy frustration. If you've ever whispered, "God, are You even watching this mess?" this is for you.

Inside you'll find raw, soul-hitting chapters like:

- "God, I Trust You — But These Bills Keep Coming"
- "If Rest Is Holy, Why Does It Feel Like Slacking?"
- "I'm Tired of Smiling So You Won't Worry"

This isn't fluff. It's real talk for real stress—and a reminder that you're not forgotten, you're being fortified.

The Faith Clinic is open. Breathe in & take your spiritual vitamins. Healing begins here.

NOW AVAILABLE:
www.amazon.com

This isn't just a feeling — it's a flare signal from the soul. You pray, serve, and believe in God, but something deep inside is still simmering. Welcome to the Faith Clinic: Anger Edition — where suppressed emotions meet sacred intervention.

In this volume, Dr. Patricia S. Tanner guides you through spiritual triage for:

- Silent rage and emotional suppression

- The grief–anger connection

- Rejection wounds from childhood to church hurt

This isn't a lecture. It's a spiritual detox. No shame. No sugar-coating. Just raw, honest healing. Whether you're snapping at loved ones or silently seething under the surface, this book meets you at the boiling point—and leads you to the breakthrough.

⚕ This is the clinic.

🔥 This is your moment.

And God is ready to heal the anger behind your amen.

NOW AVAILABLE:

www.amazon.com

In this powerful installment of the Faith Clinic series, Dr. Patricia S. Tanner brings biblical insight, emotional compassion, and spiritual strength to those walking through grief. Designed as a healing chamber for the soul, each "dose" of this devotional targets a different dimension of sorrow—guiding you from pain to peace, from mourning to joy.

Inside, you'll discover:

- Daily doses of Scripture-based encouragement.
- Personal reflections and prayers for each stage of grief.
- Practical faith prescriptions to help you process loss and find purpose.

Whether you are navigating the recent loss of a loved one, confronting buried grief from the past, or supporting someone else in their sorrow, this devotional offers a gentle yet powerful roadmap to healing. Come, take your seat in the Faith Clinic—where the Great Physician is ready to restore your soul.

NOW AVAILABLE:

www.amazon.com

30 Days Of Grieving

Given By The Inspiration Of God

Healing From COVID-19

Almost a year later, it hit me... My mother was gone, and I was still stuck at the hospital. I had tried everything from crying to counseling, and even prayer. Pray they told me. Trust God they insisted. But it seemed as if nothing was working. I was hurt, dealing with my reality: my mother was not coming back.

While journeying through grief, it was under the divine 'Inspiration of God' that He placed me in a trance. While I was gaining a revelation about grief, He gave me this journal, '30 Days Of Grieving.'

NOW AVAILABLE:

www.amazon.com

Can Salvation Get You Into Heaven? The Answer Is Yes! offers a powerful and biblically grounded exploration of God's eternal plan, revealing the heart of the Gospel and the assurance of salvation through Jesus Christ.

Unpacking life's most vital questions—Who is God? Why were we created? What does Jesus' life mean for us?—this book brings clarity to the believer's journey and confirms that salvation, once received, is eternally secure.

Whether you're seeking understanding or affirming your faith, this inspiring guide will lead you into the confidence and joy of knowing heaven is your eternal home.

NOW AVAILABLE:
www.amazon.com

The Bench That Waited is a bold and prophetic call to action for believers who've grown comfortable in church attendance but stagnant in purpose.

With raw honesty and spiritual insight, Patricia Tanner exposes the quiet crisis of passive faith—where callings are delayed and obedience is optional.

Through Scripture, stories, and reflection, this book urges readers to rise from routine, break free from spiritual stagnation, and step boldly into their Kingdom assignment. The bench has waited long enough—will you?

NOW AVAILABLE:

www.amazon.com

What happens when the Kingdom becomes a stranger?

The Godless Climb is not a rejection of faith—it is a raw, unflinching journey through what remains when belief unravels. With brutal honesty and tender grace, this book explores the spiritual free fall that follows the loss of divine certainty, the ache of unanswered prayers, and the void left when God no longer feels near.

Written for those who have quietly slipped out of the pews and into a wilderness of doubt, grief, and inner searching, this is not a triumph story—but a survival story. A confession. A sacred wrestle. Through personal reflection and prophetic insight, the author unpacks what it means to climb without a safety net, to live without the scaffolding of religious performance, and to build a new compass in the absence of old crutches.

You haven't arrived. But you're still climbing. And that is holy.

NOW AVAILABLE:

www.amazon.com

It Was The God In

Me

Success can be attributed to many things. Depending on the person who has obtained success would determine those to whom they attribute their success. Some give credit to their daily routine while others give credit to a mentor or some sort of system they followed. When I think about my success, the only person who I can give the credit to is God.

In this memoir, I share the successes and failures I have experienced throughout my life. From my individual experiences to my entrepreneurial journey, I share how God has walked with me every step of the way.

Come and see.. It Was The God In Me!!

NOW AVAILABLE:
www.amazon.com

The Triple 7 Formula is designed for business owners who are looking forward to hitting the million-dollar mark in their business. If you own a business and seem to be running in financial circles, this book will get you on track to simultaneously gaining sound business structure and millions in your bank account.

It was through many conversations with business owners lacking financial gain that prompted Patricia to share her blueprint for millionaire status. Through this book, she demonstrates how to gain financial ground by developing strong teams, implementing systems, and setting stackable goals. If you are ready to gain a laser sharp focus, and implement these clear steps, you will position yourself for financial greatness. Your business will be sound, and you will see financial growth beyond your wildest dreams!!

NOW AVAILABLE:

www.amazon.com

DR. PATRICIA S. TANNER

The Triple 7 Formula is specifically crafted for business owners aspiring to reach the million-dollar milestone. If you are a business owner feeling stuck in financial cycles, this book will set you on the path to building both a solid business structure and financial success.

This workbook is designed to complement the textbook of the same name. As you progress through its pages, you will be inspired to take decisive steps toward becoming a millionaire. From constructing your business framework to creating the millionaire's avatar, this process will expand your knowledge and mindset. Not only will you chart a course to financial success, but you will also identify your accountability circle and select a mentor to guide you toward greatness.

I cannot guarantee millionaire status unless you actively follow the steps to begin your journey. If you are searching for a get rich quick scheme, this workbook is not for you. I am looking for those ready to put in the effort—and since you are reading this, I believe that's you!

You have finally found it: Your roadmap to millions!

NOW AVAILABLE:
WWW.Amazon.com

Find Patricia on The Web:

www.PatriciaTanner.com

Follow Patricia on social media:

Facebook & Instagram: @PatriciaTannerInc

DR. PATRICIA S. TANNER